BREAKING THE RULES

VINITA GUPTA cofounded Digital Link Corporation and served as chairperson and CEO for nearly two decades, guiding the company from inception to its public listing. Digital Link was named in the Inc. 500 as one of America's fastest-growing companies. She is a board member, retired Silicon Valley CEO, writer, and international bridge champion.

She holds a bachelor of engineering in electronics and communication from IIT Roorkee and a master's in electrical engineering from UCLA. Her work resulted in two US patents in telecommunications.

Born in Lucknow, India, Vinita now resides in Woodside, California. She continues to write, compete, and explore new disciplines with curiosity and a bias for action. In her leisure time, she enjoys oil painting.

Praise for the book

'This book is a must-read for anyone navigating personal and professional crossroads. Vinita's journey unfolds with honesty, courage, and grace. I was deeply inspired by the way she transforms setbacks into stepping stones and faces each new challenge with innate curiosity. Her well-paced story is a powerful reminder of the strength found in perseverance, growth, and self-discovery.'

Barbara Tyler, former #1 realtor in Silicon Valley

'As cofounder of the leading India–US cross-border VC fund, I've witnessed countless entrepreneurial journeys shaped by the dynamic interplay between India and Silicon Valley. Vinita Gupta's story stands apart. Being the first in a foreign culture—as a woman from India—requires profound grit. This memoir is more than a reflection. It's a guide to navigating uncharted terrain in a world that's constantly evolving.'

Suvir Sujan, co-founder of Nexus Venture Partners

'This memoir reads like an adventure story because Vinita's life is an adventure. I couldn't put it down and predict you won't either.'

Danny Slomoff, PhD, author of *The Myth of Public Speaking*

'Vinita's memoir mirrors her personality: fascinating, smart, humble, yet ambitious. Her journey is refreshingly instructive in that it reminds us that excellence can be achieved while retaining and refining strong core values.'

Greg Avis, managing partner, Bangtail Partners and co-founder of Summit Partners

BREAKING THE RULES

The Road to IPO, Bridge Tables, and Beyond

A Memoir

VINITA GUPTA

WESTLAND
BUSINESS

WESTLAND
BUSINESS

Published by Westland Business, an imprint of Westland Books, a division of Nasadiya Technologies Private Limited, in 2026

No. 269/2B, First Floor, 'Irai Arul', Vimalraj Street, Nethaji Nagar, Alapakkam Main Road, Maduravoyal, Chennai 600095

ISBN: 978-937-1979-50-4

10 9 8 7 6 5 4 3 2 1

Typeset by Jojy Philip

Printed at Saurabh Printers Pvt. Ltd

Contents

PART VI
TWO TIGERS LOVE STORY

PART VII
THE DAUGHTERS

Foreword

I'VE ALWAYS ADMIRED ENTREPRENEURS. CREATING something out of nothing while following your passion is incredibly energizing. Creating a new venture while trying to assimilate into a new country is even harder. These experiences have shaped many immigrant perspectives on leadership, resilience, and the power of innovation.

Vinita and her late husband Naren were among the first Indian immigrants to take their companies public and have been a source of personal and professional inspiration. I feel fortunate to have known Vinita for over a decade and to have so many shared experiences: both born and trained in India before coming to the United States to earn graduate degrees, both veterans of established tech companies and startups alike while embracing the constant change that defines the tech sector.

In her memoir, *Breaking the Rules: The Road to IPO, Bridge Tables, and Beyond*, Vinita shares her extraordinary journey—from her childhood in India to becoming the first woman of Indian origin to take a company public in the United States. Her story is one of grit, perseverance, and reinvention. It's a tale of breaking barriers, navigating adversity, and embracing new challenges, whether in the boardroom or at international bridge tables.

Vinita's leadership style is a masterclass in authenticity. She defied stereotypes as a woman engineer in a male-dominated industry, leading with ingenuity, pragmatism, and unshakable resolve. As she recounts in her memoir, starting a hardware company in 1985 and taking it public required immense self-confidence and a willingness to embrace uncertainty—qualities that every leader must cultivate.

Her journey also highlights the importance of integrity and humility. During the dot-com crash, when many companies faltered, Vinita made the difficult decision to wind down her company's operations while ensuring that all bills were paid. This act of responsibility and respect for her employees and investors speaks volumes about her character and values. It's a reminder that leadership is not just about what you do but how you do it.

Her story is not just about business success; it's about reinvention and the pursuit of excellence in every facet of life. After stepping away from her company, she found a new passion in competitive bridge, becoming a national champion and proving that the drive to excel transcends industries and disciplines. Her ability to adapt, learn, and thrive in new environments is a testament to the boundless potential within each of us.

Stepping out of your comfort zone and being comfortable with ambiguity and uncertainty is core to entrepreneurship. As leaders, we often face the reality that not every investment will succeed, and not every decision will lead to immediate results. Vinita's memoir crystallizes this truth while offering invaluable lessons: the importance of setting a vision, challenging the status quo, and inspiring others to achieve the seemingly impossible. Her story reminds us that leadership is as much about empathy and kindness, as it is about strategy and execution.

Vinita embodies the best of Silicon Valley culture—its spirit of questioning, its belief in the untapped potential of people and technology, and its relentless drive to push boundaries. In sharing the values that guided her decisions, the lessons from successes and insights from adversity, she pays forward the mentorship and guidance she received on her own journey. Her story of resilience, reinvention, and the enduring power of belief in oneself is an inspiration for entrepreneurs, changemakers, and anyone who dares to dream.

Shantanu Narayen,
Chair and CEO of Adobe

Introduction

ON THE MORNING OF JANUARY 31, 1994, I WAS AT HOME IN Silicon Valley, thousands of miles away from where the shares of my company, Digital Link, were about to begin trading on the Nasdaq. There was no grand ceremony for me—no ringing the bell at the stock exchange, no cheering employees watching on a video feed. It wasn't the glamorous, television-worthy moment people imagine. It was ordinary. I got ready for work, kissed my children (just two and seven at the time), and went to the office, as I had been doing for years.

Yet this day was anything but ordinary. Internally, I was overjoyed, proud of my accomplishments. I was the first woman of Indian origin to take a company public on a major United States stock exchange. I had worked hard to break barriers and do extraordinary things—from going to school for electrical engineering as one of only two women in my class, to earning two patents in my name, to working in one of Silicon Valley's most innovative research labs.

The IPO (initial public offering of stock) was a milestone that resonated with anyone familiar with business and technology. It was rare air. Very few companies ever go public; they represent an elite group. As I drove to work that morning, I felt fortunate to have guided Digital Link as its CEO, overseeing the journey. Financially, the IPO changed our lives forever.

In the initial days of Digital Link, my mornings started incredibly early. I'd arrive at work at 5 a.m. to make cheap phone calls to East Coast customers before 8 a.m., or I would go to my husband's office to make product brochures on his desktop. (Portable computers didn't exist back then.) I was mindful not to be seen as 'the wife working in her husband's office during work hours.' Investors and ambitious employees shy away from family-run setups that have no room to advance and grow.

When I started Digital Link, Naren's company was just a few years old. Our kids had not yet arrived on the scene. And success—for either of us—was far from certain. The growing pains of young startups were real. Not being able to fall back to sleep in the middle of the night was common for both of us. At times, we would just get up and start playing backgammon. There were a myriad of worries to keep us awake. Would we be able to meet payroll? What should we do about difficult employees—or worse, losing key ones or partners? Then there were product delays, stalled sales, and regulatory challenges. In the tech world, there is no room to stand still.

A few years later, our kids were born. That added more structure to my day, and more joy and balance to our lives. Digital Link had grown a bit; I now had my own desktop. I began arriving at work at more reasonable hours—6.30 or 7 a.m.—but our sleepless nights continued. Now the babies kept us awake. I hired household help, even when I could not afford to take any salary home for multiple years. We learned to live with less while constantly battling everyday problems at work.

So yes, the IPO was a milestone. A big one.

Long before I ever imagined leading a company, my journey started thousands of miles away, shaped by a vastly different world. It was in Lucknow, India, that my story began. My family, though traditional, was distinctive in that both my parents were college educated. My father, a man of few words, was a civil engineer for the government. My mother, disciplined and determined (like her father), was a homemaker. My sisters and I were raised with the belief that we each had great potential and a responsibility to fulfill it. My mother in particular pushed us to enter realms normally left for men and dreamers.

Perhaps that is why I am drawn to challenges, climbing one mountain after another. As if starting and running a company while raising kids was not enough of a challenge! After Digital Link's chapter ended, bridge became the next frontier. What started as a pastime turned into complete immersion, and then a pursuit of mastery. For the past two decades, I've thrown myself into competitive bridge—with the same grit, focus, and determination.

So how did a young woman from Lucknow come to be the CEO of a successful startup and, later on, a bridge champion? This book is my story—not just of building a company, but of discovering who I am. It is a journey I am still on. In retracing my steps, I hope to share some of my acquired wisdom and hard-earned lessons with you.

I offer this book as a tribute to the little girl in 1950s India who dared to dream beyond.

PART I

IN INDIA
RAISED ON MY MOTHER'S RESOLVE

MY EARLIEST SCHOOL MEMORIES ARE FROM LUCKNOW, where I started first grade at a Catholic school run by nuns. At that time, Catholic schools in India were considered more prestigious and structured than government schools, and my mother was convinced that convent schooling would offer the best path for her girls.

My father's career made education a complicated dance. He worked for the Military Engineer Services, and like most people in service, he was frequently stationed in different cities. My entire family would move with each placement, so switching schools became a pattern in my life. Not only that, but the schools were often English-medium and sometimes Hindi-medium—meaning, all subjects would be taught in English and sometimes in Hindi. Switching between languages was hard on us.

At home, my mother placed enormous importance on our education. After all, she was the daughter of a strict chemistry professor. She taught us English, history, and geography, but if my sister or I struggled in science or math, she would summon my father, the engineer, to tutor us. She had her own undergraduate degree in English literature, rare for women of her generation. Though my father was less involved in our day-to-day studies, he took pride in telling colleagues that his daughters were attending one of Lucknow's finest institutions.

The Catholic nuns in Lucknow ran the school with strict discipline. They maintained exacting standards in everything from academic performance to personal conduct. The classrooms were orderly, the uniforms starched and ironed, and the daily routine carefully structured. This formal education left a profound impact on me as a young girl; discipline, punctuality, and neatness became ingrained.

During breaks, the veranda outside the classrooms would transform. A candyman would appear with a large metal box. It had compartments inside filled with various colored candies to sell to the children. It was a striking contrast—the strict, orderly world of the classroom giving way to an Indian street. Children would fall over each other to buy candies before the break was over.

I was two grades behind my sister in the same school, which created its own pressures. She had already established herself as a strong student, and I felt the constant, albeit unspoken, expectation to match her achievements. The nuns would sometimes reference her performance when speaking to me, adding to the weight of these expectations. My sister's presence in the school was both a comfort and an annoyance. She was there if I needed help, but her academic shadow was always over me. It only lifted when she left home for engineering college at the University of Roorkee.

Mornings began with assembly, when we would gather for prayers and announcements, overseen by nuns in their crisp habits. Lessons extended beyond academics. The smallest details—from the precise margins in our notebooks to the quiet murmur of prayers—shaped my perception of education as something intentional.

I remember the distinctive sounds and smells of those early school days: the shuffling of feet during assembly, the rustle of textbook pages, and the scent of chalk dust in the air.

The classrooms were simple but well-maintained, with wooden desks arranged in neat rows and religious imagery of Mother Mary and Jesus on the walls. Even the way we had to keep our notebooks—neat, well organized, with proper margins and headings—reflected the school's emphasis on order and discipline.

Looking back, those early years in Lucknow laid a solid foundation. The rigor of the Catholic school system, the pressure to excel, and the ever-present need to adapt to new environments would prepare me for the years to come.

The Price of Candy

MY FIRST REAL LESSON IN HONESTY CAME WITHIN THE first few months of attending school in Lucknow. Whenever the candyman came at lunch, I desperately eyed the candies, but my mother was very strict about not giving us money for such trifles. The selection wasn't extensive. They were mainly two types: chewy toffees and hard candies you could suck on. I preferred the hard candies because they lasted longer. They were shaped like orange segments and were sold without wrappers. The price was minimal—just a few paisas, a small fraction of a rupee.

At home, we had a domestic help who did the cooking and grocery shopping. My mother would give him money, and he'd return the change when he came back. Mother would then place the coins on her dressing table. One day, I decided to help myself to that change. I don't remember if I took all of it or just part of it, but suddenly I had the means to buy candies at school. I felt like a grown-up, exchanging candies for money with the vendor.

After a few days, I had more candies than I could eat by myself. Like a fool, I approached my sister during break at school. 'Didi, would you like some?' I rolled down the skirt of my uniform, revealing the candies, which I could not hold in my little hands.

'Where did you get the money from?' she asked, either suspicious or jealous—or both.

'Mummy gave me money,' I lied through my teeth.

The pattern continued until one day my mother mentioned that money kept disappearing from her dressing table. My sister spoke up. 'Mummy, do you give Nita money for candies?' she asked.

The thief was caught. My mother was furious. She was so angry that she ordered our domestic help to take me outside the community gate and leave me there. We lived in private government quarters among fifty or sixty other families. The thought of being abandoned outside was terrifying. Standing at the gate, I feared a stranger would kidnap me. Did my parents not love me anymore? After a while, I was summoned back, tears streaming down my face.

My mother thought she'd put an end to it, but the story wasn't over yet. We next moved to another town briefly and then to Bombay (now Mumbai), where I attended a Hindi-medium school in the mornings, while my sister, two years ahead of me, went in the afternoons. The vendors there sold chaat and bhel puri. My mouth would water watching the other kids eat during lunch.

Once again, I started helping myself to money from home. One day, while I was enjoying my chaat, there was a tap on my shoulder. I looked up and saw my father. He said, 'Your mummy is standing back there.'

The bottom dropped out of my stomach. I was in third or fourth grade by then, and though I don't remember the punishment, that was the last time I ever stole money.

Rather frustrated, my mother tried to instil in me that stealing and telling lies was wrong. Years later, she tried to teach me about honesty by telling me about Raja Harishchandra, a legendary king of India renowned for his integrity. She would say that whatever you say comes true if you always speak the truth like him. As a kid, this stuck in my head. Though I didn't fully grasp the lesson until later, those early moments of shame and fear planted the seeds of a deep commitment to integrity—even going to teachers when they mistakenly marked an exam paper in my favor.

When Northern Telecom became our customer, different locations would call asking for prices, and I'd quote whatever I thought appropriate that day. They never argued about the price. About a year in, while doing the invoicing, I realized it didn't make sense to bill them differently, so I standardized the price to the lowest rate I'd been charging. This helped me maintain their loyalty for the next decade. They even became our seed funders when we had no money.

Even during my time at UCLA, this commitment to honesty served me well. After trying my best on a challenging nonlinear theory exam, I simply wrote, 'I don't know how to proceed.'

The professor later told me I was the only student who had been honest—the others had fabricated their answers. He gave me an A in the subject.

Looking back, I can't pinpoint all the influences and events that shaped me into who I am today. But I do know that the little girl who once stole money for candies grew into someone who valued honesty above all else.

Extremes in Resilience

EVERY TWO YEARS, SOMETIMES MORE FREQUENTLY, OUR lives would be uprooted by my father's transfers. My mother, sisters, and I never stayed behind to finish a school year—when Daddy moved, we all moved. And these weren't simple transitions from one school to another. Each move meant adapting to a new curriculum, often with different textbooks and different expectations. I remember one instance when we had to move from Lucknow to another town, where we only lived for six months before Daddy was transferred again to Bombay. In Bombay, I attended a Hindi-medium school.

The reassignments were particularly disruptive because they often came mid-session. In those cases, my sisters and I had to wait months before the next school year began. Other times, we'd be thrust into classes already in progress and expected to catch up immediately. My older sister and I were strong students, but even then, the sudden shifts required tutors to help us catch up. The textbooks would change, new languages would be added, and at times even the medium of instruction would shift completely.

The language transitions were especially challenging. In Bombay, my sister had to learn Gujarati. When we moved to the next city, we both had to take up Marathi, a completely different language. When I reached ninth grade in Shimla, I had to choose between Sanskrit and Punjabi. I chose Sanskrit because Punjabi used a different script entirely. Each language came with its own grammar, vocabulary, and writing system. I often wondered if I would ever feel academically settled.

I used to get tremendous anxiety before each move, wondering what would change this time. Would we have to walk all alone to school? Would I be able to make friends? Before each move, we parted with our friends with teary eyes. We wrote letters to them for a while, filled with 'I miss you' sentiments, but inevitably, their lives would move on, and so would ours.

The differences weren't just academic. In Bombay, for instance, the girls wore South Indian–style clothes, while we wore dresses. Even the way we spoke Hindi had a different slant—each region had its own conversational style. These constant cultural shifts reinforced my ability to adapt. When people today worry about their children changing schools once or twice, I think about what my sister and I went through. We had no choice but to adjust.

Most of the transfers happened every two years, though there were a few exceptions. Once, my father was reprimanded for frequent absences from work. He had become deeply involved with Guruji—a spiritual leader—at the time, often missing work as a result. The civil service transferred him to a new post after just six months, a subtle but firm way of addressing the issue. Another time, we moved because they shifted the command headquarters from Shimla to Chandigarh, from the hills to the plains.

Looking back, I realize these experiences made us more versatile and able to adapt to change. I can adjust to anything now. Both my older sister and I developed this resilience, though we rarely spoke about it then. We had no basis for comparison. This constant movement was just our normal. Just as we didn't question our home atmosphere, we didn't question the impact of all the frequent relocations. It was simply the way of life for us.

Back then, my parents struggled. Life was not easy, and they often fought. At night, I would sob in my bed, overwhelmed by the fear that one day one of them might leave. What would happen to us? The tension in our household was a constant undercurrent, quietly shaping our lives even when the fights paused. But as an adult, I have come to realize that tensions and arguments are normal. Our daughters also think Naren and I fought too much. My parents are gone, but these dynamics impacted how I understand relationships now. Marriage is a complicated mix of tension, respect, and love.

My mother came from what she considered a higher-status family, and she never let anyone forget it—especially my father. She had an undergraduate degree, which she carried like a badge of honor. The conflicts often centered around her background and education against what she saw my father as—not raised in a Westernized family.

'I always wanted to work. You never let me,' she would say during their arguments, which I couldn't help but overhear. To this day, I don't know if my father truly prevented her from working or if circumstances simply got in the way. She had the qualifications—her degree in English literature was no small achievement for a woman of her generation—but she never sought out a job. This seemed to be a constant source of frustration for her.

Similarly, I remember my father's frustrations. 'You make me so uncomfortable in my own home,' he would say. 'I can't even sit the way I want because you say I'll ruin the shape of your cushions.' These issues may seem trivial in retrospect, but at the time, they would escalate into days of tension. You could tell from their faces in the morning that they had gone to bed angry, the previous day's arguments still hanging in the air.

As the middle child, I often found myself trying to mediate the situation at home. My younger sister was too young to interfere, and my older sister seemed to tune it out. But I tried to intervene, especially when one of them threatened to leave. They never left for more than a few hours—just going for walks to cool down—but in my child's mind, I feared they were leaving forever.

I was perhaps the most insecure of the three sisters, always trying to win my parents' attention. This manifested in many ways. I was the one who volunteered to help with household chores, clean up the kitchen, and assist my mother in making chapatis. I would even take my younger sister for haircuts, putting her on my bicycle—things that girls weren't typically expected to do in those days. Usually the daughters helped with the household chores, and the sons with outside errands.

More Than a Brush with Spirituality

OUR INTRODUCTION TO GURUJI CAME THROUGH MY mother's brother-in-law while we were living in Lucknow. I was six then. Technically a guru is a spiritual leader, but he also gives you the tools to deal with everyday life. This wasn't unusual in India—people often sought guidance in their struggles. Perhaps during his troubled moments, my father turned to Guruji. What started as a simple introduction would profoundly change our family's way of life.

The relationship between disciple and guru was more formal than what I understood back then. I didn't know that it involved a ceremony where the guru gives you a mantra—a sacred word or phrase. Your mantra is what ties you to your guru.

When I was in fifth grade and my sister in seventh, on the morning of Guru Purnima (a day dedicated to honor one's guru), we were asked to bathe and get dressed in new clothes. Something was special, but I did not know what. We performed our normal morning puja (worship). Then, while my parents stood around in devotion, Guruji seated my sister and me next to him and whispered a special sentence in our ears. I'm not sure if my sister heard the same sentence, as we were told not to share it with anyone. Then we were served a sumptuous vegetarian meal. The first bite was given to us by Guruji in our hands—prasad—before we ate lunch. I was puzzled by the purpose of the ritual but enjoyed that day's special attention.

After my uncle's introduction, my father became deeply involved with Guruji, spending significant time with him. My parents must have gone through the same ceremony, though we didn't witness it. I have no idea what drew my father to Guruji.

My mother never openly opposed these spiritual pursuits. When we would visit Guruji's ashram, she also joined, though I never knew her private thoughts on it. Guruji's influence soon extended beyond my father's personal spiritual journey, reshaping our entire family's way of life.

Guruji's ashram was in a village in northern India, in Uttar Pradesh, far from the urban comforts we were used to. It was genuinely primitive by any standard. Most of the children didn't even wear shoes. There was no running water, only a hand pump. There was no electricity, no flush toilets—none of the basic amenities we took for granted in the cities where my father was posted.

Guruji's compound was a hub of activity. His two sons helped manage the place. The elder one was in charge of all the farming, while one of his senior disciples managed the rest of the operations. There was a constant flow of visitors seeking blessings or guidance. On our visits, we lived upstairs in the building, becoming part of the daily rhythm of village life.

Our visits typically happened during summer vacations, when the heat in northern India was fierce. We would spend much of our time under the mango trees that dotted the property. The mangoes weren't the expensive varieties like Alphonso; they were the simple, local varieties that one could eat daily, and they provided welcome shade and refreshment in the intense heat.

I remember spending hours in those trees. While my sister wasn't the climbing type, I would climb up and hang around in the branches. She and I experienced the village differently. I was more physical and willing to embrace the rustic environment. She was more cerebral. The contrast between our city life and this village existence was stark. But as children, we adapted quickly.

Life in Guruji's village followed a strict spiritual schedule. Every morning at 6.30 a.m., we were awakened by the sound of bells for the morning aarti—a ceremony involving singing and lighting lamps. There was no possibility of sleeping through it; living upstairs, we could hear everything. After the aarti, everyone would sit and sing more hymns as the day began. The evening brought another round of aarti, followed by a more extended period of spiritual activities. People would come from other parts of the region to sing, and I remember being amazed by their talent. These weren't just religious songs. They were performances by fantastic singers who brought real artistry to the devotional music.

At first, we participated in these ceremonies simply because it was expected. I sat through them more out of obligation than devotion. But gradually, at least for me, something changed. I found myself drawn into the spirituality of it all. There was a peace of mind that came with these rituals, an ability to focus that I hadn't experienced before.

Eventually, Guruji's influence extended directly into our home life. Quite literally, I mean. He came to live with us for about ten years, from when I was in first grade until around my tenth-grade year. And when we moved from city to city, he would move as well. We now addressed him as Maharajji, which means 'a greatly respected man.' He became like a grandfather to the family, maintaining his spiritual practices while living with us.

During this period, our spiritual routines at home involved morning puja and evening puja. My older sister was recruited to perform the regular aarti at home. We all sat on the ground, participating in these daily rituals. Eventually, Guruji decided to return to his village, but his influence on our family remained strong.

I believe Guruji transformed our family in both subtle and dramatic ways. The most immediate change was dietary. We became completely vegetarian. Before that, while we didn't eat beef, we did eat chicken and, more importantly, eggs. The chicken wasn't a significant loss since we only had it once every few weeks, but the eggs were a daily breakfast staple that my sister and I really missed. We used to fuss about not having eggs anymore, though I can't remember what replaced them in our morning routine.

Thankfully, Guruji's presence eased some of our parents' tensions. While their conflicts over status and education never disappeared entirely, the spiritual practices and Guruji's serenity introduced a different energy into our home. My father's complete devotion to Guruji was so powerful that my mother had little choice but to accommodate it, even if she harbored private reservations.

Guruji's influence also left a lasting impression on our worldview. My sister and I often reflect on how, because of his teachings, we never saw anyone as beneath us. In his village, we were surrounded by farmers and laborers—people without formal education or fluency in English—yet we were taught to touch their feet as a sign of respect. When we married, we carried this mindset with us, refusing to look down on anyone.

Even after we became the only working women with engineering degrees in our families, we held on to that principle. I carried it forward as the CEO of a public company. Thanks to Guruji, I've never felt superior to anyone, no matter what their job or social status is. When I hired executives in my company, I showed utmost respect. I believe my direct, honest approach—which others noticed but I was not as consciously aware of—came partly from that early spiritual immersion. My executives responded to this authenticity. It developed mutual trust, which made the path to solving problems easier.

The impact Guruji had varied among us three sisters. Interestingly, my youngest sister, who was quite young during this period, was the most influenced by him in the long term. Perhaps because she experienced it differently, coming to it later than we did and viewing it through different eyes, she developed the strongest spiritual connection. She still prays and offers food to gods first before eating herself—like we all did back then. She leans on spirituality when faced with problems.

Personally, the experience gave me something different. While I never mastered meditation or became deeply observant, life with Guruji taught me about inner peace and finding focus amid chaos. When people talk about meditation techniques today, I have to laugh. I was introduced to meditation as a seven-year-old and still can't do it properly. But my inability to meditate doesn't negate the spirituality it instilled in me.

Engineering at Roorkee

ROORKEE WAS ONE OF INDIA'S MOST PRESTIGIOUS engineering colleges at the time, and remains highly respected today. My mother was the reason I ended up there. She had decided that my sisters and I would go to Roorkee since my father had studied there. When I was considering colleges, going to the even more prestigious Indian Institute of Technology (IIT) wasn't even discussed. (Roorkee was not part of the

IIT system then.) My mother had such high esteem for my father despite their conflicts. She thought he was brilliant and handsome. These were the two things about him she always maintained. My father had gone to Roorkee, so in her mind, that was where we should go too.

I think part of her reasoning was also because, in India at that time, a woman who didn't bear a son was considered a failure—and in our family, it was just me and my two sisters. Not having a son was never seen as the man's fault. My mother was determined to prove that her daughters were as capable as any sons. While other families with daughters focused on accumulating money for dowry, she decided that wouldn't be the case for her girls. She wanted us to be married, of course, but education was her number one priority.

Roorkee had a distinct character that set it apart from other colleges. Founded by the British, their influence could still be felt in its traditions and expectations. We had to wear formal attire, dine in the hall with forks and knives, and dress up for Saturday evening dinners. Yet, it wasn't just a rigid and formal institution—Roorkee had vibrant extracurricular activities, including a photography club, swimming, various sports, and opportunities for leadership roles.

My path to Roorkee was not straightforward. I spent an additional year getting in because my final exams in high school and Roorkee's entrance exams fell on the same date. Hence, I couldn't appear for Roorkee's entrance exams the year I graduated, so I had to go to another college for that year. During that year, my father was transferred once again. That meant I needed to retake the finals because it was another board in another state. In the meantime, they said I could continue taking that current year's college classes.

Unfortunately, I mistakenly thought my chemistry lab exam was scheduled for a month later than its actual date, so I missed it. My father had some influence in the small town, and my mother asked him, 'Sahabji'—she addressed him the way Guruji did—'Can you do something about it?' Ultimately, I was allowed to take my chemistry lab exam late, avoiding wasting another year. That wouldn't have mattered if I got into Roorkee—but what if I didn't?

At that time, very few women majored in math and science at the university level. I ended up choosing electronics and communications because that's what my sister had done. She was already at Roorkee, and when it came time for me to choose my subject, I thought, *Oh, that sounds good. I'll also do electronics.* Admission was based on one's entrance exam performance, and I was fortunate to get in and get my preferred choice.

The engineering program started with a common curriculum for everyone. Whether majoring in civil, mechanical, or electronics engineering, all students in the department had to learn the basics of every engineering discipline in their first year. In my year, Roorkee's entire electronics class had only two women out of twenty-eight students. Three-quarters of all the girls at Roorkee went into architecture, with only one-fourth choosing engineering.

Early in my first year, a mechanical engineering professor called me and the other woman in our class, Rashmi, into his office. 'I am like your father,' he said. 'I advise you not to waste two spots in this excellent engineering college. You girls will be married off, and these are valuable seats.' He was implying that married women would not be able to pursue a career in engineering. We heard him out but left his office dismissively, shrugging off his words. Both of us have worked throughout our lives—Rashmi in India, and I in America.

My years at Roorkee were full of challenges and rebellion against a deeply conservative system. Most engineering professors were uncomfortable with female students. They would not even look us in the eye while teaching and would only address the rest of the class. There was one exception—a female professor who taught semiconductors. She was different, probably because she was also a Roorkee graduate and the wife of another professor. She was the only one who interacted with us normally, unlike the male professors, who maintained their distance.

The conservative atmosphere extended beyond the classroom. Roorkee hired a young woman as our sports coach for the women's swimming class. She was five or six years older than us and always wore a sari. Standing at the pool's side, she would say, 'Extend your arms like this and kick with your legs.' She never got in the water herself. I figured out that she didn't actually know how to swim, and in the end none of us learned to swim because nobody was teaching us. Her instruction was all theoretical. She would also take a few girls aside and boast about her supposed boyfriends in the army barracks nearby. Then, she would ask us not to tell others.

The women's swimming competitions at Roorkee were comical. There would be one girl here, another there, along the other edge of the pool. And our coach, who couldn't even swim herself, would time us. It was very entertaining. They put curtains on the barbed wire fence around the pool so boys couldn't watch us swim. I could swim better than the others, so I won. But it was hardly a real competition.

We also had yoga classes taught by a male instructor—maybe the only young man who came regularly inside the women's dorm. When it came time for the yoga competition, they invited the vice-chancellor's wife and other professors' wives as judges since men weren't permitted to see girls doing yoga. We wore loose pants called salwar to maintain modesty. No shorts.

During the final competition, the instructor had a favorite student he wanted to win. The class had to do a pose called the plow (Halasana). For the plow, you lie down, put your feet up to touch the ground behind your head, put your hands to touch the toes, and then bring your feet back very slowly without bending your knees. It's very hard on the core. I realized the dignified wives, in their dignified sarees, who had perhaps never done yoga, wouldn't be able to tell if I bent my knees or not (or they might not know that was the hard part). So I cheated. As you can tell, the path to honesty and truth, for me, was imperfect at best. I won the competition, much to the yoga instructor's annoyance. He knew what I'd done.

During my third year, I led a strike in the dormitory over the quality of the food. Most girls constantly complained that the mess food wasn't worth the money we were paying. While I personally didn't care much about the food, I saw an opportunity. My classmate was positioning herself to become the mess leader, while I was aiming to become the dorm leader.

Food expenses were a significant concern for students and their parents, so we decided to strike—refusing to eat in the mess. To sustain ourselves, we organized shifts among dorm mates to cycle into town and bring back food. Each trip, we would bring meals for twenty-five to thirty girls. We continued this routine for several days—until the warden complained to the dean.

At Roorkee, we had something called discipline marks controlled by the dean of the university. A student could lose a year if they did not get passing grades in all courses—including discipline. For leading the strike, I could have been detained by the dean for a year. When the warden told him who the strike leader was, I was called in for a meeting, and the dean threatened to expel me. I was near the top of my class and doing well in other activities, so the threat was serious. I couldn't risk being expelled, so the strike was called off, but by that time we had made our point. The warden was apparently warned because the food eventually improved. The following year, I became the dorm leader, and my friend became the mess leader.

Each year, we had an annual show in the dormitory. We invited all the professors along with their wives. The girls would participate, and we'd all put on a big production. This always included a slideshow—often about poor food quality or poking fun at the warden. As the dorm leader in my senior year, I decided to include slides about our sports coach, exposing her boyfriend stories. Some worried she would know who was telling on her, but I reasoned that she had told the stories to so many girls that she wouldn't remember who knew what.

These weren't my first times challenging authority. In eighth grade, when I attended a boarding school run by nuns, I led a different rebellion. It was the Hindu god Krishna's birthday (Janmashtami), and we wanted to celebrate like we did at home with puja. The nuns said no, citing Prime Minister Nehru's rule regarding no religious functions in dorms. I decided to wait and see how they handled Christmas. When the day came and the nuns went for night prayers, we took out our pictures of Hindu gods and the bell the nuns used to signal study times. We sang Hindu religious songs in Hindi, not realizing how far the sound would carry in the silence. When the nuns discovered us, we all ran to our beds. They threatened to write to our parents, but nothing ever came of it.

I had a tendency to rebel against authority when something was clearly wrong. I was bold as a girl and as a young woman. That has continued to this day.

A reason girls tended to go into architecture over engineering was the physical strength engineering required at times. As mentioned, all first-year engineering students had to take workshops in every type of engineering craft: carpentry; civil engineering surveys, where we measured heights and distances; and foundry work, making sand molds and pouring metal. I remember struggling with my sand mold box. It was so heavy I could barely lift it onto the table after getting the foreman to pour the metal at ground level. The professor would inspect it at the table, and I was too proud to ask for help from male classmates. So foolish!

A mandatory subject was mechanical drawing, requiring us to draw three-dimensional perspectives of objects. That meant visualizing the objects from an angle. I simply couldn't do it. When I asked my sister, who was still at Roorkee then, she said, 'It's easy.' And she sketched it. She was good with visualization, just like with math. I finally mastered mechanical drawing through hard work.

I also involved myself in various activities at Roorkee. I joined the photography club and learned to develop pictures in the darkroom. I even won a photography competition with a photo I took using my father's camera—a playful picture of him with my one-year-old cousin. I also continued oil painting, a hobby I became fond of after attending a summer program in high school. Once, I asked my department head at Roorkee if I could display my paintings during a conference. To my surprise, he agreed, and visitors to the electronics department were able to see my paintings alongside their technical discussions.

Despite all these activities, I remained focused on academics. I was consistently second in my class, always struggling to beat the top guy but never quite managing it. He probably worked harder, while I was involved in so many other things. I cared about more than just school work; I wanted to excel in other areas too.

My best friend during these years was Rita, an architecture student who studied constantly. I don't know if she ever slept during the four years I knew her. She always ranked first in her class, and I drew inspiration from her dedication. When I got involved in dormitory politics, she discouraged me, saying, 'Why are you wasting your time? It adds no value.' But I did it anyway. She went on to become a professor at the University of Chicago, moving away from pure architecture into healthcare-related fields, while I became a businesswoman.

The Last Summer in India

LIKE MY CHOICE OF COLLEGE, MY PATH TO AMERICA WAS guided by my mother, not my father. She was bent on proving to the world that her daughters were no less. I overheard conversations with one of her sisters, who would take pity on my mother for not having sons. Among the female cousins on my mother's side, my older sister and I were the only ones who became high-level professionals.

My father's sisters, who were all older than him, grew up in a much more traditional household. One married after sixth grade with little education but then went on to get a PhD while having children, eventually becoming a college principal. Another sister was educated and became a professor. She never married and, later in life, became a disciple of one of the Gandhians. I remember overhearing my mother say, 'I don't want my daughters not to get married like you.' That was the first time I realized she expected us to marry. It was never mentioned before or after. She wanted us to do it all: to get married, have a career, and have children.

Going to America was what all the best IIT graduates did back then. America offered a much better financial future, especially within engineering. I applied to several schools, but UCLA was the top choice because my sister was settled with her husband in Los Angeles and already enrolled at UCLA. Those were the days without internet, and telephone calls from India to the US were prohibitively expensive. Applications were done by mail, and a fee had to be paid with each application, which was quite expensive. I didn't even know about the existence of Caltech or Stanford then—nobody at Roorkee had told me about them.

While getting ready to depart for America for further studies, my parents continued looking for potential matches for me. I met several prospects. Then they responded to a matrimonial advertisement Naren's parents had placed in the *Hindustan Times*, a newspaper with a huge circulation and the most popular one for matchmaking. Our fathers corresponded, and soon the next traditional step arrived.

It was a hot summer day in June 1973 when he and his parents came to our house to meet me and my parents. Since it was so hot and we had no air conditioning, we all sat out on the balcony—a confined space. I was excited. My heart would always beat faster when I first met a new prospect. Naren and I sat there and talked for two hours, always within earshot of our parents. Not that they were listening in—they knew better.

Back then, couples were always chaperoned by their parents for the first few meetings. You didn't go for a walk or on a date. That was not how it worked. Usually, in that kind of setting, the girl is shy and the guy stiff. But I liked Naren's relaxed demeanor. Talking to him was like talking to a friend—easy and effortless.

He wasn't reluctant to show he was interested in me. Often, in those circumstances, a suitor talks about esoteric subjects because it's too awkward to show any interest. Naren wasn't put off by the setup. He was smooth enough to have a natural conversation with me, unbothered if anyone else was listening.

I don't remember exactly what we spoke about that first time, but he was warm and friendly. I liked his casual style of talking and laughter. He was clearly intelligent and knew how to listen to what I had to say. Neither I nor my parents were influenced by his degrees from Caltech or Stanford. We were totally unaware of rankings of colleges in America. But his highest ranking in Delhi's IIT entrance exam impressed me!

After a few hours, Naren's family left. 'We'll get back to you,' my parents told them, thanking them for their visit.

After they left, my parents asked what I thought.

I said, 'Don't worry about me. I haven't fallen in love with him. I've just met him once.' I had my emotions in check. I wasn't going to get carried away. It was my way of deferring the decision to them.

Internally, I was torn. Did I want to get married right away? Or did I want to go to the US to pursue my studies?

My parents were also of two minds, but I had the feeling they were leaning toward me going to California for my master's degree. So we talked it over, and that became the family decision. My parents thought he would be an excellent match for me, but once we decided on UCLA, arrangements had to be made, and soon it was time for my flight.

My parents did not immediately get back to Naren's parents. Eventually, my father made that call. It was awkward for both sides, so he delayed delivering the news as long as they politely could. I left India at the tail end of that summer of 1973, still single.

PART II

IN AMERICA: UCLA, MARRIAGE, AND LEARNING PROFESSIONALISM

I ARRIVED AT UCLA WITH THE SINGULAR GOAL OF completing a master's degree. My parents had invested their savings into my education in America, and I was acutely aware of their financial burden. Determined to minimize costs, I set out to complete the program in just nine months.

Initially, I had considered bioengineering, but when I learned that it required a thesis and would extend my time in school, I decided against it. I couldn't afford to stay another quarter or two. In my third quarter, I managed to secure a non-resident tuition waiver, significantly easing the financial strain. I had seen an advertisement for the scholarship and asked my adviser to write a letter of support. That small victory brought relief to both my parents and me.

Despite the tuition waiver, money remained tight, and I knew I needed a job immediately after graduation. Midway through my second quarter, I began searching for work. The process was far more challenging than I had anticipated, primarily due to my visa status. I was on a student visa, which allowed me to work for eighteen months after graduating. Most companies were reluctant to hire someone with a temporary visa, and as a result, I did not receive any on-campus interview opportunities.

The contrast between my academic success and professional uncertainty was stark. I maintained a perfect 4.0 GPA, but this achievement felt hollow when faced with the practical challenge of securing employment. While I excelled in my coursework, I watched my classmates smoothly progress through on-campus interviews, building their futures one meeting at a time. That path was not available to me—my visa status meant I could only interview off campus.

My job search intensified in the third quarter as the reality of my situation set in. The career center became my lifeline. This was pre-internet, and the process was painstakingly slow. I carefully scanned newspaper postings, taking down company names and details. Without even a phone to make calls, my only option was to send letters—a method that felt like sending messages in bottles into an ocean of uncertainty.

The Interviews

THE CHALLENGE WAS NOT JUST FINDING JOB LISTINGS; IT was understanding an entirely foreign system of employment. In India, prestigious jobs were secured through competitive examinations, typically leading to government positions. The private sector was minimal, and few companies hired engineers directly. Most of my peers either pursued further education or competed for government roles. In America, I faced a system

I could not decode. I had no idea what made candidates employable in private companies or how they would evaluate me outside the familiar framework of competitive exams.

Despite these challenges, I secured several interviews in Los Angeles. The aerospace industry was thriving at the time, and Teledyne invited me for an interview. Since they did not cover travel expenses, I took multiple buses to get there. After the interview, I was informed that I would have to sit in a room for a year doing nothing before they could assign me work since 'we do classified work here.' It was unclear why they had called me for an interview in the first place. Employers were not particularly knowledgeable about visa restrictions at the time.

A pivotal moment occurred when I was in the career center, scanning job postings. My professor walked in and asked what I was looking for. I hesitated—I was in no position to be selective. At that time I would have accepted any engineering job. It turned out that he had consulted for GTE Lenkurt, a company in the Bay Area, and had sent other students there before. He made a call to them on my behalf, and soon I had an interview scheduled.

The company offered to pay for my airfare and car rental, but this presented a new challenge: I did not have a driver's license. I had driven in India, but my brother-in-law in Los Angeles refused to teach me, fearing I might get into trouble in a new city. My cousin in Los Angeles also declined to help, likely after consulting with my brother-in-law.

With no other options, I turned to Rashid, my dorm mate from Pakistan. I needed to rent a car, so we went to Hertz—the only rental company I knew from television advertisements. It turned out to be the most expensive agency, but I had no time to make comparisons.

Rashid had recently obtained his license and was familiar with the test route used by the California DMV. He took me there and had me practice the maneuvers he remembered. After a short while, he was visibly nervous. 'Stop, Vinita! That's it.' He was sweating. I never knew if it was my driving or his nerves, but he was relieved to take the wheel back.

Soon after, I took my actual driver's test while Rashid waited at the DMV. The instructor marked off a few points, but I passed—having driven for just half an hour in America. Both Rashid and I were so delighted that we hugged each other, and I treated him to a hamburger at McDonald's. It was a happy moment, both for him and for me.

Just a week after getting the license, I went for my interview with GTE Lenkurt, located in the heart of Silicon Valley in San Carlos, California. My first act was crossing a picket line. Manufacturing workers were on strike, and as I approached the plant for my interview, I had to pass the protesters. As a new immigrant, I did not think much about it—I badly needed a job.

The interview process was particularly memorable. The human resources (HR) representative treated me with notable respect, though I later understood this was largely due to my professor's recommendation. After the interviews concluded, they made me an offer that same day. I was excited, overjoyed, and relieved. It took a big burden off my shoulders. Fourteen thousand dollars a year was more than what my father was making after working as an engineering executive for twenty-five years in India. I would finally be able to ease my parents' financial burden.

Securing my first job was not just about employment—it was about decoding an entirely new system of professional advancement. Each challenge forced me to adapt and learn. I could not figure out life all at once, but I could tackle it piece by piece. And my transition was not only professional—it was cultural and personal. Looking back, I see how those early struggles shaped my approach to everything that followed. Each letter I sent, each interview I attended, and each obstacle I overcame built the foundation for my future success in Silicon Valley.

Although I did not realize it at the time, being different—being the only woman, the only immigrant, the only one excluded from traditional recruitment channels—would ultimately become a source of strength. It taught me to find my own path when conventional routes were unavailable. Or perhaps the strength came from the adaptability that became ingrained from my father's frequent job transfers, when our school curriculum changed overnight and I had no choice but to adjust.

What stands out most in my memory is the HR representative at GTE Lenkurt giving me specific instructions with the letter of offer: 'Don't discuss your salary with anybody. You will be the highest-paid fresh graduate.' At the time, I accepted this as another rule to follow. Today, I recognize it as a standard tactic companies use to manage wage disparities and avoid disruptions. But back then, I was simply focused on navigating the unfamiliar terrain of corporate America.

Marriage

WHEN NAREN HAD VISITED OUR HOME WITH HIS PARENTS, he had jotted down the name of my brother-in-law. Soon after my arrival in America, Naren called and asked for me. This was our new start.

While I was completing my degree, my parents were still looking for matches for me. By this point they were searching for a suitable young man already in America. The parents of these men would advertise in India just like Naren's parents did, and that would be the start of the process. My parents would urge my sister in Los Angeles to invite the prospects to her house to meet me.

Several young men were invited, and my brother-in-law and sister chaperoned the visits. We would typically go to a botanical garden in Arcadia and then have dinner somewhere before the men were sent away. One prospect was a professor from Colorado who was too dull for my tastes. Another was very charismatic, but he was not interested. Maybe he was looking for someone more beautiful—I wasn't as attractive as some prospective brides.

Meanwhile, Naren wrote me a letter at UCLA, using the electrical engineering department address. We started exchanging letters, which increased our fondness for each other, though we had only met once in India.

When other prospects did not quite work out, my parents requested that my brother-in-law invite Naren. This was at the tail end of completing my degree at UCLA. So we met again—same botanical garden, same routine. It was warm and friendly on both sides. But we stayed in wait-and-see mode. No decisions were made on that visit either.

Eventually, I graduated and moved to the Bay Area for my first job. This carried the added attraction of being closer to my potential suitor. I rented an apartment within walking distance of Naren's, and we spent nearly all our free time together. We went to the theater, and he introduced me to his friends from Stanford. I became part of his circle, and as we grew closer, we both felt more and more certain that we wanted to build a life together.

Within six months after graduation, in 1974, we got married in a small ceremony in my sister's backyard in Arcadia. The marriage solved my long-term work visa problem also—Naren had a green card and was on his path to citizenship.

My First Job

I BEGAN MY CAREER AT GTE LENKURT IN JUNE 1974, stepping into the world of American corporate culture with little understanding of its nuances. Barely a month after I started, the company had its annual shutdown—a two-to-three-week period when all employees were required to take their vacation. As a new hire without accrued time off, I was one of the few still coming to work, along with other trainees and those who hadn't accumulated enough leave. It was during this quiet period that I began to grasp the character of my new workplace.

GTE Lenkurt was a traditional telecommunications company, deeply rooted in analog communications infrastructure. It was not a hub of innovation (by today's standards) but rather a steady, established firm focused on microwave equipment—hardware that interfaced with FM radio and frequency-modulated infrastructure. While the technology was not cutting-edge, it provided me with a solid foundation in electronics manufacturing. I gained firsthand experience in designing and producing electronic products tailored for corporate communication.

As part of a first-year rotation program, I was exposed to various aspects of the company's technology and production processes. This broad overview helped me understand the telecommunications industry at a time when digital technology was still emerging. Digital was the future, and everyone wanted to work in it. My professor had warned me against specializing in filter design, believing it was becoming obsolete. He was right—analog systems were gradually being replaced, and the shift toward digital would define the next three decades of technological evolution.

One of the most impactful rotations was factory support. Sounds mundane, but I enjoyed it. Unlike design work, where projects could remain unfinished for months, factory support required immediate problem-solving. The impact was very tangible, and I found it gratifying. If an issue wasn't resolved, production halted. Production delays then delayed shipment, which meant delayed revenues.

During this time, I witnessed a pivotal moment in computing: The introduction of the first widely used 8-bit microprocessor. This marked a significant transition from analog to digital, leading to the development of personal computers and minicomputers. In telecommunications, it meant faster, more efficient systems that consumed less power. The industry was evolving rapidly, and I was eager to be part of that transformation.

The social dynamics at GTE Lenkurt were, at times, perplexing. Even though I was told that I was the first woman engineer GTE Lenkurt had hired, I met two other women, who said they were engineers in the company. Linda, a chemical engineer, worked on thick film hybrid layouts—a specialized niche that kept her somewhat separate from the main engineering teams. The other woman engineer stood out in a different way, with her dramatic makeup, fake eyelashes, high heels, and short skirts. She was Korean. There were whispers about her relationship with a manager in another group. The gossip was constant, and while I found it amusing, I also saw it as a distraction from the work at hand.

After completing my rotations, I was assigned to a group led by Bob Tracy, widely regarded as the company's most brilliant mind. His team worked on digital interfaces with analog systems—an area at the forefront of telecommunications at the time. Bob was exceptionally intelligent but painfully shy, which made our work relationship challenging.

After a year of what I believed was strong performance, I received my first review. Bob gave me an average raise. I had never been average in my academic life, so why now? There was no explanation, no discussion of areas for improvement—just a number on a piece of paper. I wondered how I could become a top performer in an environment where feedback was so minimal.

Looking back, I see many signals I missed that indicated I was considered a promising engineer at GTE Lenkurt. Typically, engineers who were going to a competitor were asked to pack and leave immediately. When I announced my departure, however, the vice president of engineering took an unusual interest in me, asking why I was leaving.

GTE Lenkurt had been a great starting point, a soft landing in the American corporate world. But the culture did not prioritize intellectual rigor or forward-thinking. When I left for Bell Northern Research, I knew I was stepping into a more dynamic environment, one that would be better for my technical growth.

The Bell Labs of Silicon Valley

BY 1978, BELL NORTHERN RESEARCH (BNR) HAD BECOME one of the most sought-after workplaces in Silicon Valley. Though their Palo Alto office was barely two years old, they had quickly established themselves as a hub for ambitious engineers. At GTE Lenkurt, BNR was frequently mentioned as the place to be. I watched a steady stream of our best engineers leave. They were drawn by the promise of working on cutting-edge technology.

Unlike legacy companies that were slow to adapt, BNR had strategically positioned itself in Palo Alto to tap into Silicon Valley's growing talent pool. They were willing to pay for top engineers and, more importantly, offered an environment that encouraged innovation.

When I started exploring the possibility of leaving Lenkurt, Rick Faletti, a senior staff engineer at Lenkurt, had already moved to BNR, and he offered to be my reference. His endorsement carried weight; he later became a VP at Northern Telecom, the parent company that funded BNR. His willingness to recommend me was another significant validation of my work.

The interview process at BNR is a blur in my memory, but my first day stands out vividly. As I sat in the lobby, Al Boleda, who had been a senior engineer at GTE and would later become my boss, made a special appearance just to meet and greet me. It was a small gesture, but significant.

BNR had a different approach to hierarchy. Titles were minimal; we were all simply members of the scientific staff. My initial assignment placed me under Wayne, who introduced me to Sam Wood, my supervisor on BNR's most ambitious project: the office communication system (OCS). The goal was to develop a next-generation PBX (private branch exchange) to compete with digital products from Mitel and ROLM. The system architecture was complex, involving a backplane with multiple cards—CPU memory, peripheral cards, line cards, and trunk cards.

Sam Wood was uniquely valuable to BNR. He had an intricate knowledge of how AT&T's central offices interfaced with customers' phones or data modems. Much of these interface designs were undocumented—perhaps intentionally. AT&T did not want other companies making phones and connecting them to their central office. I was hired to design the line and trunk interface cards for the new OCS system under Sam's supervision.

BNR's work environment was a stark contrast to Lenkurt. The culture encouraged intellectual exploration, and the atmosphere was dynamic. Engineers were constantly experimenting with new ideas, both for work and personal projects. Unlike the rigid office politics and gossip at Lenkurt, BNR fostered a hacker mentality—rules were seen as suggestions, and barriers were challenges to overcome.

Lunchtime bridge became a ritual. I regularly played with Inez, the only other female electrical engineer at the company, along with Jim Locke, a well-known hacker. One day, Jim casually said, 'I know your salaries now.' When we asked how, he smirked and said, 'I hacked into the BNR Unix payroll system.' He was only mildly reprimanded—they didn't allow him to touch Unix computers in the company. BNR was very employee-friendly. This was the essence of BNR. The excitement around new technology was palpable, and many of my colleagues spent their spare time building projects in their garages.

Patents and Promotions

I WAS NOW WORKING FOR MY BRIDGE FRIEND, INEZ AREND. Inez was an exceptional leader, an engineer's engineer, widely respected for her technical expertise. She had fled Prague with her family in 1939, escaping the Nazi takeover, and later became the first woman to earn a master's degree in electrical engineering at the University of Santa Clara. She was fifteen years older than most of us. She dressed casually in pants and a top, like most BNR employees, and was easy to talk to.

Inez was a supportive boss. One day, she encouraged me to apply for a $50,000 research grant from Bell Canada headquarters. 'No harm in trying,' she said. 'It's for three months.'

I applied. The decision came fast. May be it was BNR's pace of decision-making, or perhaps Inez lit a fire under them. A month later, Inez told me with a big smile that Ottawa had approved the grant. I was delighted. It was an opportunity to shine at BNR, but what could I work on? I only had three months from start to finish. Scientific research projects take far longer to do anything significant.

I started with the line card interfacing with AT&T that I had already designed for the PBX. There was the large switch sticking out on it, equivalent to an electrical switch in a home. But it was electromechanical—for automatically switching high voltages. AT&T sent -48 volts over connecting wires to the old black phones in homes to detect when a customer lifted the handset to dial a call. On their end, AT&T then switched to connect a shared receiver to detect the dialed number. I thought, why not attempt to design a digital switch instead? And that is what I succeeded in doing. That was my invention!

A digital switch has many advantages. It can be laid on a semiconductor chip, which are cheaper, faster, and more power efficient. That meant the PBX interface card to AT&T could become all digital. It also meant future phones might become all digital, like we have now. The new digital era was on the horizon. That would become the foundation of my company Digital Link, five years later.

BNR recognized the value of my invention and brought in an intellectual property attorney from Canada to work on my patent. I had no idea BNR had a patent department, let alone that they would invest resources in securing intellectual property for my work. This is when I thought, *Now I will shine.* It was a big deal for me. When the attorney arrived, he was in awe of me. I was also perhaps the first woman filing for the technical patent at BNR. He realized that my work was not just technically significant—it was breaking barriers.

The patent process was straightforward, and soon my invention was officially recognized. BNR offered to fly me to Ottawa in early 1982 for an award ceremony for my first patent. A few years later, I was awarded a second patent in conjunction with a brilliant engineer. It was an all-digital tone detector. When we press numbers on a modern phone, different tones are sent for different numbers. At the AT&T end, they detect them and connect them to the dialed party. But Matt did most of the heavy lifting on that one.

The patents were more than just a recognition of my work. It was a turning point that pushed me to think bigger and take risks. It instilled in me the confidence that I could do things that I had never done before. Ultimately, it prepared me for when I would start my own business.

Around my third year at BNR, an opportunity arose that would change my career trajectory. I was asked to prepare a presentation on PBX traffic engineering for a new vice president. The presentation explained how many line cards were needed to connect to trunk cards based on traffic patterns. Naren provided some insights, though he was characteristically brief with his assistance. He was a systems-level engineer. But after a tiny bit of discussion with him, my understanding improved dramatically.

The VP, who was three levels above me, was impressed enough with my work to advocate for my promotion to first-level manager. When I was promoted, Herb Steierman, who would later become my business partner, decided to join my group. This is when we came in closer professional contact. Herb had also been at GTE Lenkurt when I was there, and we used to go out for Friday lunches with our group. Naren and I started socializing with Herb and Steve—another Lenkurt engineer. Steve and Herb were good friends. Steve and Naren started playing racquetball over the weekends, followed by breakfast at either Steve's place or ours. Herb also joined us.

Herb was friendly but a bit private. He was tall and thin with closely trimmed curly hair. Despite my initial concerns, Herb showed no reservations about working for somebody who was his peer. He was easygoing, a self-starter.

As a new manager, I had no say which team members I got. Wilson was one engineer I 'inherited,' and he was known for his real estate dealings. In our open office with cubicles, everyone could hear each other's conversations, and Wilson's side business was no secret. When he was consistently behind in his assigned project, I went to HR to learn the proper procedure for terminating him. They explained the importance of documentation—assigned tasks, feedback given, and performance reviews—to create a paper trail.

Following their guidance, I ultimately fired him. This was unusual at BNR, which had a reputation as a cushy company where managers rarely fired nonperformers. Years later, I ran into Wilson at a bank. To my surprise, he approached me and said, 'Vinita, one of the best things you did for me was fire me. Now I just do real estate and make a lot more money.'

Another time, I allowed my direct report, Jim Locke, to prematurely send his design for layout on printed circuit board (PCB), after which changes are hard to make. One had to cut a trace on the PCB and put a jumper wire across to the right point. Only two PCB revisions were allowed per card due to the high costs involved. My boss had a strict limit of ten jumpers maximum on the first go around of the PCB, but I allowed Jim many more, knowing he would eliminate all of them in the next revision. That was how Jim worked: careless at first but smart when push came to shove. It saved the company time and added no extra cost.

However, from the expression on my boss's face as he looked at the spaghetti of jumpers on the first PCB, I could tell he was annoyed. And when Jim cleaned it up completely in the next revision, he did not turn around to compliment Jim or me. But sometimes doing what's best for the company means breaking rules.

PART III

THE STARTUP BUG

THREE YEARS INTO WORKING AT BNR, A CRISIS OCCURRED that caused a change in the work environment. We'd been working on the OCS, the new system that would involve cutting-edge digital technologies and be far more powerful than our old SL1 PBX. But now we faced a devastating technical reality: When you picked up the phone, it took a minute and a half to get a dial tone, even under light traffic conditions. We had been developing the OCS as different subsystems in isolation, and it turned out that they didn't work well together.

A couple of weeks later, an announcement came for an all-hands meeting. BNR rented a hall, catered with food, drinks, and beer—a common practice then. A new Northern Telecom executive, Dave Twyver, appeared with other familiar faces. As mentioned, Northern Telecom was the parent company for BNR. They were the sales and marketing arm of Bell Canada—the 'Ma Bell.' Twyver delivered the bad news: 'We have made a decision to cancel the OCS, but there will be no layoffs.'

We were in tears. Our baby, which we'd worked on for years, would never see the light of day. Twyver then said, 'In the coming weeks, a new project will be announced.'

Bob Kelsch, our quiet but brilliant boss, was likely at the meeting, though he said nothing. In the two weeks after we discovered the technical problem, Bob was quietly transferred to Northern Telecom.

Bob Kelsch had fostered an environment at BNR that prioritized technical excellence. Outcomes were emphasized over process, and risk-taking was the norm. His replacement brought a more bureaucratic approach. The change wasn't immediate, but it was significant.

The new project we were assigned was an enhancement of the old SL1 system, very underwhelming after the system we'd been working on. Had Bob not been sidelined, he would have pushed for a newer, more creative technology. However, innovative technology had inherent risks.

By my eighth year, BNR's transformation into a dysfunctional workplace was sadly complete. The dynamic and driven organization I'd joined had become something else entirely. Projects took longer, decisions grew more complex, and the spontaneity that made BNR special faded. When I asked myself if I could be happy in this environment for another five years, the answer was clear: It was time to move on.

The final straw came in September 1984. Our boss had interviewed me and another co-manager for promotion to the next level. I was delighted for what looked to be the next progression in my career.

Naively, I assumed that because I'd constantly put company interest first, including painstakingly firing a nonperforming engineer, I was head and shoulders above the other guy. Also,

I had made great efforts to save the company money when traveling to BNR headquarters in Ottawa. I always bought the cheapest ticket and traveled after hours to maximize my work time there. I told this to my boss, Al Boleda, when I was passed over for the promotion. But it was too late. He had announced the decision.

I felt totally dejected. The very next week, I decided to tender my resignation. It was scary—I had no clue what I would do next, and my biggest fear was becoming a regular housewife. But I just knew I had to leave BNR. I gave eight to nine weeks' notice, wanting to finish all my projects and make a clean break. It would have felt horrible sneaking around during workdays for interviews or planning sessions, as most people did.

At my farewell luncheon at BNR, people kept asking what I would do next. 'I honestly don't know,' I told them. My first thought was to move to marketing; I was going to explore that first with other competitive companies. In those days, starting your own company was much less common than it is today.

Many expected and unexpected BNR friends showed up at my luncheon. Herb, my long-term buddy from my first job at GTE and now at BNR, also came to my lunch. Finding a quiet moment, he said, 'Vinita, if you ever want to start a company, give me a call.' I didn't give too much attention to his words at that moment, but things were beginning to happen.

After quitting BNR, I gave myself a strict ninety-day deadline to figure out my next step. Naren hadn't been entirely comfortable with my decision to quit without a plan, but he provided practical support. He gave me an office in his company's building while I considered my options. The office environment gave me a base from which to explore opportunities and eventually plan Digital Link. Working from home wouldn't have given me the drive or motivation to search inside myself and decide on what I wanted to do.

I sat in Naren's office for three weeks, contemplating my options. I interviewed with some telecom companies and voice messaging firms, but Herb's offer kept coming back to me, even when I wasn't trying to think of it. Sitting in that office, a blank slate before me, I was able to look at my choices more clearly. When I compared the idea of starting a company with my other options, I realized that this was the best path.

At the end of three weeks, I called Herb. We met at Harry's Hofbrau in Redwood City. Over roast beef sandwiches, we began planning what would become Digital Link. Of course, first we spent time bashing BNR—how it was too bureaucratic and political, and how hard work wasn't rewarded.

Herb shared that his parents had a lighting fixture store in Phoenix. 'I worked there one summer,' he added. 'Making money in a business isn't so hard, Vinita.' Those words were reassuring, but I also thought he was a bit naive to compare a low-tech mom-and-pop business with a technology startup. Still, that lunch opened my mind to the possibility. What we didn't discuss was what product we'd actually sell!

The early entrepreneurial environment at BNR influenced everyone who worked there. Sam Wood was a prime example. He had a uniquely valued technical expertise, and BNR tolerated his openness to other ventures. That also engendered creativity in the rest of us. During our potluck lunches and social gatherings, conversations would often turn to starting companies or new ventures.

Naren and I would socialize with my BNR colleagues in our relaxed home environment, where ideas got tossed around.

Naren, I believe, became influenced from this and started his own company. Sam Wood helped Naren install his office PBX system, accepting only lunch and dinner as payment. I even got that system purchased, at employee discounts, from Northern Telecom. These experiences showed us how BNR engineers truly embraced entrepreneurship, something we hadn't felt from regular Americans before. The culture made us more optimistic and more willing to listen and participate in new ventures.

I used Naren as a sounding board for my next steps. I explained that my two options were to work elsewhere in marketing or start my own company. But I was concerned—'How can we have two startups at the same time?'

He replied, 'What's the big deal?' It didn't faze him. His words gave me a boost, launching me toward my own business.

The next time Herb and I met, we had product discussions. During the first bake-off of potential products, we considered two options. The first was my idea, and ambitious: a simplified version of BNR's abandoned next-generation PBX system designed for smaller offices. We thought we could succeed where BNR had struggled by creating a product for small offices that wouldn't support as many lines. Having witnessed BNR's difficulties firsthand, we believed we could design a better, simpler system that would cost less and be easier to use.

However, as we analyzed the requirements, reality set in. A PBX system, even a simplified one, would require multiple types of cards, hardware, software, and integration elements. It would require significant parts. The complexity wasn't just technical—it was financial. We had no idea how to raise the necessary funding to build a prototype. Herb correctly said, 'We can't do it on our own.' We were just BNR and Lenkurt people—engineers who understood technology but not venture capital.

The second idea came from Herb's BNR experience with T1 cards. T1 cards are network interface cards (NICs) that allow devices, like routers or PBXs, to connect to the phone company. They are capable of carrying twenty-four voice or data channels at a rate of 1.544 megabits per second. Herb knew that PBX T1 cards needed an external box to connect to the phone company; no one could connect directly to the phone company's network without it—it was a regulatory requirement.

Herb also knew how to design the box, and quickly. He was very familiar with T1 specifications, as well as the competitive boxes already on the market. Another important consideration was that, unlike the PBX system, T1 cards would not require nearly as much capital, and Herb already knew the ins and outs of the technology. Moreover, this way we wouldn't be competing with BNR; we would be complementing their products.

This was a golden opportunity, as T1 lines were just emerging as a popular service. The traditional model of having multiple voice lines between locations, each incurring toll charges, was becoming expensive and unwieldy for large businesses. And while the internet didn't exist yet, large companies were beginning to think about digital com-munications. The timing seemed near perfect.

An exciting moment came when we decided on a company name. At first we considered Gupta-Steierman, but we favored a name that included 'digital', as it was the start of a digital era. Herb liked 'link' because our product would 'link businesses to AT&T,' the phone company. When our attorneys researched and found 'Digital Link' available, we were very happy.

Herb and I looked around for models for our startup. We both liked the example of Hewlett-Packard (HP), which was a hardware company as well as a software company. Everyone viewed HP as a model enterprise with deep roots in the Valley. You always hear about Steve Jobs and Steve Wozniak starting Apple Computers in Jobs's parents' garage in Los Altos. HP was also started in a one-car garage in Palo Alto—on New Year's Day in 1939.

Bill Hewlett and David Packard began their business making equipment to test electronics. Their big break came when they landed a contract to provide eight audio oscillators to Walt Disney for its production of the animated classic *Fantasia*. The rest, as they say, is history. That famous garage on 367 Addison Avenue now carries a plaque designating it as the 'Birthplace of Silicon Valley.'

By the time I arrived in the area, HP had grown into a large technology employer famous for its strong employee culture. 'The HP way,' as it was called, was often cited. That meant managing by walking around and offering advice or assistance. When the company's profitability suffered during the recession of 1969 and 1970, HP avoided layoffs by asking employees to agree to reduced hours and pay by 10 per cent, which they all did. In six months everyone was back to working a full schedule. This strong culture made an impression on me.

In March 1985, two months prior to launching Digital Link, Herb and I met for our first official 'business' meeting in the office Naren had given me. My new space had a desk, clean carpets, and even a window. I wasn't yet grounded in the reality of used furniture and the stale carpet smell I'd later face when we rented our own space. At the moment, we had no customers or contract work, and the reality was stark. We agreed we'd have to put money into the company and wouldn't take salaries for at least six months. The big unanswered questions were how we'd build our product and how much money we'd need. Economic anxieties quickly surfaced: Herb was unmarried, while I had some financial cushion from Naren.

Herb looked at me from across the desk. 'What if you decide to have a kid?'

'We've tried,' I assured him. 'It's not happening.'

Herb and I were in sync, but we had some obstacles to overcome. A conflict soon emerged around organizational structure. I insisted we needed formal titles—maybe just to set his expectations. Herb resisted strongly, citing his parents' successful lighting fixture business that operated without titles. The discussion became heated. I argued that while two partners might work without titles, we needed a clear structure when hiring others. Employees needed to know who did what and who made decisions in what areas.

After much debate, we decided that Herb would be VP of engineering and I would be president. (CEO wasn't a common title then.) But this led to an even more contentious issue: salaries. Herb insisted that since we had invested equal money, we should receive equal salaries. I countered that equity and salary were different matters. While we each would take 70–80 per cent of our BNR salaries (and these would be accrued, not paid, as we couldn't afford actual salaries yet), we each would have the same equity. I explained to him that equity was shares you own in the company. Salary was what you earn. The two were different forms of compensation. While the exact salary difference was minor, it became a point of principle. Naren, with his business experience, helped explain why titles and salary differences were important, but these early discussions created underlying tension that never fully resolved.

Starting a hardware company is very different from creating a software or consulting business. You can run a software startup from your bedroom with very little overhead—just a few thousand dollars, a server, and a laptop. Your employees can work out of their kitchens or (in the Valley) garages. You have the flexibility to scale up when you can afford to scale up. However, software products are often much more labor-intensive than hardware products, and they can expand to near infinity.

A hardware company requires far more upfront investment. Long before you have your first customer, you have to rent space, buy materials, build inventory, buy test equipment, and develop products—and that's before you even get your first sale. I tapped our savings to put up $25,000 of our own money, which was all we had. Herb put up another $25,000 (including his IBM personal computer).

I was shocked to find myself going down this path. At the time, I thought I did not have any business sense, whether in making financial statements or negotiating. The idea of taking significant financial risks was antithetical to everything I'd known so far. I never dreamed I would even contemplate starting a company, let alone actually do it. Growing up in India, my father worked as an engineer in the military. Military families like ours tended to look down on business people, considering them greedy and less intellectual—that was just the culture. Now I was a business person. I had to make a serious adjustment in how I saw myself. I was glad my parents were not here to dissuade me.

We opened our first independent office on University Avenue in Palo Alto, a happening location for early startups. Every aspect of starting the business brought new lessons. Having worked as an engineer in large companies with their own purchasing departments, I had never purchased electronic components myself. It was an altogether new experience. I needed to buy parts to make a trial batch of twenty-five boxes. Back then, everything was on the phone, and I called up a representative of the electronic-parts distribution company, Hamilton/Avnet, as it was then known. This was the same company that in 1973 became Intel's first supplier.

I explained to the woman on the phone what I needed and made clear that, as a startup, we would need to keep costs down. 'Well,' she told me, 'I can give you a 10 per cent discount.'

That was not much, and it wasn't going to work for me. 'How can you offer me only a 10 per cent discount?' I asked. 'What do you give Cisco?'

'They're a high-volume client,' she said. 'I don't know what discount they get, but I'm sure it's 40 per cent or more.'

It was a catch-22. We could only get a discount if we were big. But we could only get big if we had the discount.

'If you don't give me the same discount as Cisco, we'll never become big,' I said, partly appealing, partly demanding. It was my first time trying to negotiate.

There was a pause. 'Let me talk to my boss,' she said.

We hung up, and I wondered if I would ever hear from her again.

An hour later, my phone rang. 'Okay, you can get a 40 per cent discount,' she told me.

Somebody at that company clearly understood the importance of taking a longer view. To help small companies become big, you make some sacrifices in the near term to set yourself up for sizable earnings when that company grows and becomes a loyal customer. At every step of the way during those first few months, we unexpectedly found people willing to help us. The landlords, office furniture sellers, and PCB designers were all willing to offer us discounts.

Then people like Dick Elkus, a business savvy executive, would not hesitate to drive to my office to assess problems and render advice for free. Even new employees, who knew we could not pay market salaries, were willing to negotiate. I don't know if a startup can make it without that help. In Silicon Valley, everyone wants to participate in the entrepreneurship ecosystem in their own way.

Naren recommended reputable attorneys to help us set up the company and register it with the state. It had to be done the right way. However, four months in, they sent us a bill for four or five thousand dollars for sending us fair employee practices documentation. Good attorneys do things proactively to protect the company, but we only had two employees, both of whom were founders. We didn't need this type of documentation, nor could we afford to pay hefty legal bills prior to selling a single product.

Herb was adamant: We're not going to pay anything. I had to explain to our attorney, Fred, that we didn't have employees yet and couldn't afford these fees. Thankfully, Fred agreed to retract the billing.

The contrast with our BNR experience was stark. At BNR, everything was departmentally structured. There were clear roles, departments for every function, and support staff. Now, if the phone rang, one of us had to answer it. If a customer needed technical support, one of us provided it (usually Herb). If a shipment needed to go out, one of us had to package and ship it. This experience was invaluable—learning by doing is very different than being taught in a classroom.

Herb proved to be remarkably efficient, designing and delivering ten boxes in less than four months. This pace made us both laugh when we compared it to BNR, where it would have taken a year and a half just to introduce a single card.

However, our hardcore hacker engineering mindset, carried over from BNR, led us to scrutinize every component. Did we really need this resistor? Did we really need this line header or this extra LED? We took out anything that was not absolutely necessary. This attention to detail and cost would later surprise customers—our product was so light that one potential customer picked it up and asked incredulously, 'Does it have anything in it?' Compared to our competitor Verilink's much heavier boxes, our Digital Link box was light as a feather.

Everything was a bootstrap operation. If something needed doing, one of us had to figure it out. We found contract manufacturers who would stuff and solder our printed circuit boards, but we did all testing in-house. Thing was, we could not afford expensive testing equipment. When Herb asked how we would test the product, I had to design a test fixture myself so that we did not have to buy or rent expensive equipment. This hands-on approach ensured quality control but also meant long hours and constant problem-solving.

Marketing materials was another challenge. I was not a marketing guru and had no experience writing marketing copy. Still, I did my best. We had no budget for professional design, so I found a creative solution. At 5 a.m. each morning, I would go to Naren's company, almost next door on University Avenue, and use their TeX typesetting software to create a print-ready brochure. It wasn't a work of art—just a simple brochure that got the message across, explaining Digital Link's product in telco-speak. I also took out an advertisement in the newspaper, which we got zero leads from. I soon learned what should have been obvious: You did not advertise enterprise technology in a local newspaper.

When our first brochure was ready for printing, I went to the printer across the street on University Avenue.

'Do you want two colors or four?' they asked.

Despite the price jump from $300 to $1,000—a fortune for us then—I chose four colors. We needed to look professional, like a real company, even though we were two newbie engineers starting from scratch. I knew we had to compete with fancy marketing teams without having a marketing department or even a marketing person. Spending the money on a brochure was the least we could do.

Then came our masterstroke. In July or August of 1985, we managed to acquire BNR's sales directory and did a mass mailing to their salespeople. Our message was carefully crafted: This is designed by ex-BNR engineers and works perfectly with the T1 interface of an SL1 PBX. We weren't competing with BNR; we were complementing their product. We didn't want to ruffle feathers. And we were fulfilling what we believed was a real market need. We had heard as much from salespeople at Northern Telecom.

We got our first leads from this mailing, and we soon became an approved product that BNR would co-sell to customers alongside their bigger PBX systems. BNR's parent companies became one of our most important accounts. They even installed Digital Link products to run inside BNR's internal networks to save money and streamline the deployment and management of data and voice lines.

After the sales directory caper, I was on a roll. It wasn't so much having all the right words as it was making sure you were talking to the right people. Years later, Airbnb's founders pulled a similar trick when they scraped apartment and vacation rental listings from Craigslist and sent the owners emails pitching a better way to make money from their properties. Some tactics are timeless.

I began attending trade shows and carefully collecting competitor information. I'd typically conceal my identity as I gathered brochures from companies like Verilink and Adtran. When I found Verilink's reseller list on the back of their brochure, I started contacting them. I then planned a trip to the East Coast to meet with these resellers. I had no idea what I was doing, and the sales trips were exercises in startup humility.

In New York City, I met with an Italian reseller in the cafeteria of the World Trade Center. (It was still standing then.) Neither of us offered to buy coffee for the other. I didn't know enough to offer. He looked at our brochure and asked some questions. I figured it was a waste of time, but he later became a good channel for us.

In Rhode Island, I met with a one-person telecom equipment reseller who was very entrepreneurial. He was the one who taught me about channel economics. I mentioned that our planned price was $500 to $600. That was less than half the price of Verilink's product.

He laughed and asked, 'How are we going to make any money at such a low list price?'

'Well, what should we charge?'

He explained that a reseller earned 15 per cent of the price of the product. Obviously, they would rather sell Verilink's product, where they made a lot more money. But if we set our price a little lower than Verilink's, it would make sales easier without hurting the reseller's pocket too much.

He suggested a price roughly 20 per cent below Verilink. I did the math quickly in my head. That would give us among the highest margins in the industry! That seemed crazy! But the reseller knew the market. He said, 'The right price is not the lowest price—it's the price that would motivate a reseller to move product.'

So I had to learn about reseller margins and adjust our pricing strategy to do a better job taking care of an important customer: our resellers.

How would an engineer at BNR know this? Founding a company in real life was invigorating but also complicated—it wasn't something you could learn by reading a bunch of case studies, hiring consultants, or going to business school. And it was about to get even more challenging.

As mentioned, a breakthrough came when Northern Telecom's internal offices started buying our T1 modems. Bart, a friend at Northern Telecom, helped us acquire formal approval that it worked with their systems. This certification became crucial for our startup funding. As one location would buy our boxes, others would follow. It was just enough revenue to bring the next meal to the table.

Our relationship with Northern Telecom grew organically and was driven by actual demand for Digital Link products—not relationships or favoritism. I was very proud that the parent organization of BNR valued my company's products enough to refer us to their customers and deploy them in BNR's own internal networks. We could not have asked for a stronger endorsement.

Another turning point for Digital Link was securing FedEx as a customer. Their name carried weight, symbolizing reliability and operational excellence. Having FedEx on our customer list instantly elevated our credibility, signaling to potential clients and investors that our product met the rigorous standards of a global powerhouse. But the way we won FedEx—and nearly lost them—taught me one of the most valuable lessons in business: the importance of rebounding.

In startups, setbacks are inevitable. Products fail, customers reject them, and deals fall apart. But how a company responds to failure—how quickly and effectively you rebound—often determines its long-term success. Rebounding is not just about persistence. It's about learning from setbacks, adapting swiftly, and using those hard-earned lessons to drive forward. In the conservative telecom industry, where reliability is paramount and risk tolerance is low, the ability to recover from early missteps is critical.

A couple of months after Herb finished designing our product, a Northern Telecom salesperson happened to mention Digital Link to FedEx, noting that we were founded by former Bell Northern Research engineers. That was enough for FedEx. They called us and placed an order for all eight of our evaluation units—our entire inventory. For us, this was a significant order, nearly $10,000. For FedEx, it was a rounding error.

We were both jumping out of our chairs. Herb was so excited that he rushed home to get Bubble Wrap to pack the units safely. I called FedEx to confirm the shipping method (perhaps a silly question). Of course, they provided their FedEx number and requested overnight delivery. For a startup, landing a customer like FedEx was a game changer. The FedEx logo on our reference list would do wonders.

A week later, I followed up, eager to hear how the products were performing. 'We haven't installed them yet,' Ron, our contact at FedEx, replied.

I was baffled. Why had they requested overnight shipping only to let the boxes sit unopened? Another week passed. When I called again, Ron seemed annoyed. 'Same answer,' he said.

After another week, at Herb's urging, I called Ron again. This time, he said in a serious tone: 'We tried installing them. Your product does not work. I'll be shipping them back.' My heart sank. I rushed to Herb's office to deliver the bad news.

We decided to call Ron together. 'The engineer who designed the box is on the line with me,' I told him. Ron had no idea that I was the CEO and that Herb, the engineer, was VP of engineering and cofounder.

Ron described the problem, and Herb calmly assured him that he would be there the next day to fix it. Herb got on a plane, arrived at FedEx, and quickly resolved the issue. Ron was impressed—not just with our product but with our swift response. Herb, in his straightforward style, probably shared with Ron that we were only a two-people company.

After Herb's visit, Ron called me and said, 'Feel free to use my name as a reference.' It was a massive accomplishment on Herb's part.

This was my first real experience with sales. I thought good products sell, and that was that. But now I understood what rejection felt like—and sales people face it every day. I also learned that my priorities were not my customers' priorities.

Ron had other things to do, but I kept calling, anxious to see our product installed and tick off a win for Digital Link.

This was our first rebound, and it was pivotal. We nearly lost a major customer, but we responded with urgency, which larger companies often don't. This is a reason customers buy from smaller and more hungry startups. Our focus on the customer and ability to rebound turned a failure into a win.

As a new founder, I had assumed that better features and lower prices always won. I quickly learned that trust and relationships matter just as much. Rebounding—recovering from setbacks, adapting swiftly, and earning back customer confidence—became a crucial ingredient in my journey, ultimately helping to take Digital Link to an IPO.

Losing One Oar

IN SEPTEMBER 1985, FIVE MONTHS AFTER WE'D STARTED the company, I returned from one of my sales trips, elated about potential reseller agreements. I found Herb sitting quietly in the office. There was no 'howdy' from him, like other times. After I made coffee, he came into my office. I was anxious to give him the trip update, but Herb clearly had other plans.

With a serious expression, he said, 'Sorry, Vinita, but I've decided to quit Digital Link.'

My jaw dropped. 'Really? What happened, Herb?'

'Nothing.' A pause. 'I've thought a lot.'

'We can talk it over.' I looked at him, my heart pounding. 'Tell me what I need to do differently.'

He frowned. 'I can't take you anymore.'

That was quite damning and hurtful. We had started off well. So far, we'd been able to share every concern. Perhaps in the heat of starting a company, he had grown unhappy, but I didn't want to believe it was beyond repair.

The next morning, when I came in, I went to his office on the other side of the wall, hoping he might have cooled down. But no. His firmness left no doubt that he hadn't changed his mind.

I sat in my office and thought about what I might have done differently. Ultimately, I decided 'not much.' I immediately called Naren to get his thoughts. The previous night we had talked, and he advised me not to shut down the company. He offered now to meet us both for lunch, but Herb refused. I felt dejected.

Once Herb and I got over the hard part, our parting was relatively calm. He could not keep any of his shares due to the four-year vesting period that our lawyer had wisely included in our agreement. However, since I couldn't pay his accrued salary, we agreed that he keep 25 per cent of his shares as collateral.

Herb seemed surprised that I would want to continue, and in truth it was a bold moment for me. Now alone, I had to find an engineer and dole out cash from my pocket. I put a small advertisement in *The Mercury News* and hired a technician, Tom. He was versatile and convinced me that he needed no benefits—just a job.

Though relieved to have found Tom, I had to become more creative to stay profitable. I started adding shipping and handling charges to our invoices—$20–$24 on a $1,000 product. This was pure profit. All large equipment companies added charges like this, so we were not doing anything that other companies weren't doing. But it mattered. Every bit of margin mattered because the high margins helped us take the company public and quickly helped us become—and remain—cash flow positive for the vast majority of the company's lifespan.

With gross margins exceeding 50 per cent, we were shortly bringing in $30,000 to $40,000 monthly in revenue. This was enough to pay bills after offering below-market salaries to employees (which startups make up for in stock options). I still couldn't pay myself, though. Slowly, we grew sales and expanded our product line. The growth was not a hockey stick, but it was steady and strong, and our high margins held steady. Our survival was no longer the big question. It was more about how we would grow and what kind of company Digital Link could become.

Two years into the venture, Tom Perkins, senior partner of Kleiner Perkins, visited our office to see if he wanted to invest. I showed him our little operation and the books. He was a well-poised, elderly statesman, yet he showed admiration for what I had accomplished with Digital Link. I had spoken a few times with potential investors and VCs by then. They had shown interest, but not the curiosity and kindness I saw from Tom. I felt he treated me with utmost respect, and although he ultimately decided not to invest, he gave me interesting advice. Tom told me to try and pay Herb's unpaid salary, if I could, and get back the shares he was holding per our parting agreement. Tom explained that having a large chunk of equity in the hands of a departed founder could make it harder to raise capital and fund the company later on.

I contacted Herb and offered to show him our books. We were making a little money, though not enough for me to pay myself yet. I offered to pay Herb the six months of back salary Digital Link owed him if he would honor the agreement and return his shares. He agreed. I took pride that I'd acted on Tom's advice. Before he spoke to me, I was unaware of the issue. Now I owned almost 100 per cent of the company (a small number of shares were granted to the employees).

Each day brought new challenges and lessons. I was on a journey from engineer to entrepreneur, discovering that technical excellence was just one part of building a successful company. Over the years, as I first raised a venture capital round and then took Digital Link public, I was increasingly grateful for Tom's wise words.

Early Employees—The Heroes

AFTER HERB'S DEPARTURE, BUILDING THE RIGHT TEAM became my biggest challenge. My first employee, Tom, was an optimist. His role was testing and troubleshooting products for shipment, but he said he could do a lot more. 'I can do engineering and marketing, and go to trade shows too,' Tom would say. While he couldn't truly engineer products, he became our jack-of-all-trades, useful in many ways. He provided a certain comfort factor in my tiny operation, helping with testing, support, and whatever else needed doing.

Finding reliable engineering talent proved particularly challenging. Our second engineering hire, Scott, exemplified this difficulty. He lived in Scotts Valley near Santa Cruz, a long drive from Palo Alto. He usually rolled in around 11 a.m. with elaborate explanations about how he had been thinking about a project he was working on. Scott's references had been stellar. His previous startup even claimed he kept working after they stopped paying him. In retrospect, this might have been less about dedication and more about his inability to find other work. When questioned about actual progress, Scott would launch into particle physics-level explanations. This was his way of obscuring his lack of productivity. He could talk big game, but couldn't deliver results. I had to let him go within six months, as soon as I found a replacement.

Curtis Wright became our first dedicated sales hire, though he wanted to be considered a sales executive rather than just a salesperson. Like most of our early employees, he came from a startup. Curtis was memorable in several ways. He was honest and polished, and I noticed that he delivered bad news in two chunks: 'I'll tell you more about customer X.' Then, a few days later: 'Customer X decided to buy from Verilink.' I still use this approach, as people adjust more easily to the news this way.

One day, he told me that I needed antiperspirant. He approached the topic carefully and with great respect. 'It is very embarrassing for me to even raise that with you,' he said. 'It may just be a cultural difference.' I realized when I wore polyester shirts, I smelled of perspiration. I had never heard of deodorants or their usage in India. I didn't mind his honesty and thanked him. It must have taken guts to tell me.

A couple of years later, I hired Mike Rico as the first manager of manufacturing. The day Mike came, I never had to lock the doors again when I left for the day. He relieved me of managing manufacturing and facilities. It was a big relief.

Unfortunately, Mike resigned within a few years. I had hired someone in a leadership position over him, and a few months later he decided to leave. The production had gotten too large for Mike to manage, and the parts were not arriving in a timely way due to lack of coordination. When Mike resigned, I had tears in my eyes.

Every hire in those first days was a bit of a misfit of some kind. They had to be if they wanted to join such a small, unproven company with an unusual immigrant CEO. Early employees don't usually treat founders as godlike; they don't hesitate to challenge them just as they would a coworker. This was a new dynamic for me. 'I reported to Eric Benhamou, founder of 3Com,' one might declare. Some comments were plain embarrassing: 'I'm attracted to you—do you feel the same?' or 'Can you man the booth while I take this young chick out for a drink?' As a woman from India, I was shocked. But I learned about American egalitarian culture in a hurry.

These early hires who thrived in the startup chaos often struggled as we became more structured. They enjoyed the multiplicity of their tasks, walking with heads held high: 'I can do marketing, selling, and hiring' or 'I can do engineering and marketing.' This versatility was incredibly useful for saving money in a startup. I myself was like that and appreciated it.

However, as we grew from five people to ten to fifty, it became clear that some early hires were not scaling with the company. They either couldn't work in teams or weren't communicative enough. Through these early experiences, I developed a reputation for being quick to fire people—perhaps too quick, as some would later say. I couldn't tolerate inefficiency, carrying over my frustration from BNR, where inefficient employees were tolerated for too long. When people weren't performing, I quickly told them it wasn't working out. Obviously, that can cause real problems when the decision to fire a longtime employee is not clear-cut and obvious.

By 1987, two years into the start of Digital Link, I'd learned that success requires understanding your people—their strengths, weaknesses, and motivations. Early employees might be misfits in traditional companies, but they could be valuable contributors if managed correctly. That was how we got the most bang for our buck in the early stages. The key was identifying who could grow with the company and who would eventually hold it back. I naively thought people who joined would stay with the company forever. It took time to understand that different stages of growth require different types of people.

Founders deserve credit and praise, but so do the adventurous employees who join shortly thereafter. Although founders often capture the headlines, it is the early employees who truly fuel Silicon Valley's innovation engine. The roles of these dedicated individuals are chronically overlooked. They accept pay cuts and commit to longer working hours amid significant uncertainty. And they undertake these sacrifices not purely for equity or the chance to become wealthy. (Everyone in Silicon Valley knows that employee stock options are somewhat of a wild card.) Instead, these fast-following employees choose startups because they relish the freedom of an unstructured environment where experimentation is encouraged. They enjoy the thrill of creating something new and different. As a founder and CEO, I have personally witnessed this dedication.

Tom, Curtis, Scott, and Mary—four of my earliest hires—had previously worked at startups that ultimately failed. Some hadn't even received the salaries they were promised, let alone gained financial success. Yet to join Digital Link, they again accepted below-market salaries, forfeited job security, and willingly embraced uncertainty. While they valued their stock options, their motivation was not solely financial. More significantly, they were drawn by the allure of building something entirely from scratch and the opportunity to make a genuine impact.

When hiring, I sought passionate people because I wanted them to share my excitement about building something meaningful. Each hire, from my very first to my eighth, brought unique skills and a steadfast commitment to launching the company and turning it into a substantial success. They willingly stepped outside the defined boundaries of their roles and stretched beyond their initial capabilities. Some, like Tom, even oversold their abilities. As a first-time CEO, I wanted to believe in Tom's claims because how could I afford to hire separate individuals for every specific role? In essence, they took a chance on me just as much as I took a chance on them.

Venture Funding

BY LATE 1987, APPROXIMATELY TWO AND A HALF YEARS after starting Digital Link, I faced an important decision: whether to sell the company or not. Dynatech, an East Coast conglomerate based in Virginia, offered to buy us for $2.5 million. I traveled to West Virginia to meet their senior executives, including the head executive, who ultimately made the final acquisition offer. Dynatech wasn't just any acquirer. They specialized in purchasing smaller technology companies and operating them as independent subsidiaries while providing centralized management and resources. Their acquisition strategy focused on steady companies rather than those exhibiting explosive growth. The $2.5 million would be distributed according to our equity structure, which had changed after I bought back Herb's shares.

While considering Dynatech's offer, our connection to Summit Partners through Naren's company opened another door. Greg Avis from Summit regularly attended Naren's board meetings and was familiar with my progress. When Summit learned about Dynatech's offer in late 1987, they presented a counteroffer: They would invest $1 million at a precise $5 million post-money valuation, acquiring 20 per cent of the company. Summit believed we had a bigger future ahead, not merely steady performance, and they were investing their own money and taking on considerable risk. I also believed Summit could provide valuable expertise and connections to help me elevate Digital Link to the next level.

Naren and I discussed it thoroughly. Summit had invested in his company as well, and he had positive experiences with them as investors. Ultimately, we agreed it made sense to accept the venture capital and bet on ourselves. Dynatech's offer felt like a nice compliment, but accepting it would have implied that I couldn't grow Digital Link independently. I didn't believe that at all—I still had the ambition to expand the company and eventually take it public.

We finalized the terms of the deal with Summit. But I had also just found out that I was pregnant—some long-awaited good news for Naren and me. That was mid-1987. I felt Greg Avis, our venture capital partner, should know, and I asked Naren, 'Can you tell Greg that I am expecting?' I was too shy, given my Indian upbringing.

Greg immediately called to congratulate me. This struck me for two reasons. The first was that in India people never congratulated you on news of a pregnancy. It was not part of the culture. The second was that I had not fully allowed myself to feel the joy of the moment yet. Internally, I was battling how to handle the precarious situation of navigating venture funding while being pregnant. Just those thoughts made me choke for a few moments. But now I had to face this challenge. Would Greg agree to move forward or not?

He did not cancel our next scheduled meeting. After small baby talk, Greg asked, 'How do you plan to take care of the baby and run a company?'

'I guess I will hire help,' I said.

And that is what I did. The concept of a nanny was not as common in those days. Mothers hired au pairs or babysitters. In all of Silicon Valley, there was a total of one nanny agency: Mothers in Need. I contacted them, and they informed me that most nannies wanted immediate employment, so I had to wait.

The timing for all this was significant. I became pregnant in mid-1987 and gave birth to Anneka in March 1988. The negotiations with Dynatech and then Summit also started in mid-1987, and the venture capital deal closed just months before Anneka was born. Negotiations with Summit were extensive and detailed; having Dynatech's offer gave us leverage. Summit's investment proposition was compelling because it not only valued the company higher than Dynatech's offer, but it also allowed us to maintain control and build toward a potentially much larger exit. During these negotiations, we discussed everything from board composition to reporting requirements and growth expectations.

In January 1988, while seven months pregnant with Anneka, I attended a telecom industry trade show in Washington DC, to meet one of Summit's limited partners. Greg had arranged the meeting specifically, saying, 'We want you to meet one of our LPs.' The LP was a French investor, though at the time, I didn't even understand the meaning or role of an LP in venture capital structures.

After the meeting, the LP asked Greg if he knew I was pregnant. Greg laughingly told me that he'd said, 'Of course!' It emphasized that his trust in me and my leadership hadn't wavered. I loved the vote of confidence, and Greg remains a close personal friend today. We were fortunate that our investors became more than mere business associates—they became our friends.

In the deal, Summit also included a $500,000 payout to me. Summit had their reasons for providing me with financial security, but I thought they were being overly generous. I had worked tirelessly for three years to build the company without taking a penny home. When they handed me the money, Greg humorously remarked, 'This will buy some shoes for the junior.' This payment wasn't intended to keep me at the company—I had no intention of leaving Digital Link. My motivation for starting the company was hardly financial; I was committed to building something lasting. And now I was committed to proving Greg's investment in me worth his while. The money certainly helped me to focus fully on the company.

After the venture funding, we were moving on to the next phase of our growth. Part of Summit's expectation was that I build a senior management team. I had never been a VP myself, and I had no clue what to look for in them.

The type of individuals I hired for my executive team joined because, to them, 'small was beautiful.' The VP of research and development, Dan Palmer, told me, 'When I came in for the interview, the company lobby reminded me of a dentist's waiting room.'

Curious, I asked why he then chose to join us. He responded enthusiastically, 'But that is exactly what I was looking for!' He came from a highly successful company where the CEO ruled with an iron fist. After that company was sold, he wanted to stay in the Bay Area and decided to work for me. I had no particular gravitas or executive experience, similar to him, and my style was apparently a breath of fresh air.

Someone I knew had provided an unsolicited glowing reference for Dan. I grew rapidly as a CEO partly by seeing him operate. He was truly a lucky find, a fast learner who interacted well with customers and never hesitated to meet them personally. He was a good listener, readily admitted his mistakes, and had the courage to embrace startup risks even though he had a young family and stay-at-home wife.

When we began hiring senior executives, we had the venture capital funding, which allowed us to offer more competitive salaries. Additionally, we provided employee benefits—not as comprehensive as those at established companies, but significantly better than in previous years. However, the challenge remained that I had never been an executive myself, and felt inadequately prepared to evaluate and attract senior talent.

Yet, those senior executives joined us anyway. Despite their impressive résumés and extensive industry connections, they were drawn to an uncomplicated CEO like me. Later, they shared that my authenticity as a boss was a significant part of my appeal. Both our early unconventional employees and experienced executives were driven by the shared desire to create something extraordinary and challenge the status quo. For the executives, the startup world offered a unique opportunity to shape the future; this justified the personal risks they took. As CEO, I felt deeply responsible toward my executives and all the employees. I did not want to disappoint them, so I worked diligently for them, and they reciprocated with equal commitment.

The startup ecosystem is propelled by these unsung heroes—both the early junior employees and the bold, risk-taking executives. They labor tirelessly, often without proper acknowledgment, to transform innovative ideas into reality. We all shared the common goal of seeing the enterprise succeed, and like me, they were dreamers.

With the half-million-dollar payout by Summit Partners, we moved from our small home in Menlo Park to a larger house in Atherton, investing virtually all of the money in this move. The Atherton's zip code is consistently ranked as the most expensive in the United States. Naren and I used to eye this neighborhood on our bicycle rides, wondering if we would ever be able to live in that neighborhood. And now we were here.

A month before Anneka was born, we hired Julie as our nanny. She was a Scandinavian woman in her thirties with fair skin and blue eyes. Julie came across to me as a loving and caring person. Just three weeks after Anneka was born, I returned to work, leaving my newborn in Julie's hands. This wasn't an easy decision, but the demands of Digital Link required my presence, particularly as we navigated toward becoming a public company.

Julie formed a deep bond with Anneka, often commenting on her brown eyes, dark skin, and straight black hair. She would say that the boys would be falling all over her. They enjoyed playing board games together as Anneka grew.

Moving to Atherton was a wise decision, as it enabled Julie to live upstairs. In Atherton, we stood out distinctly: We were the only Indian family and the only household with young children in a neighborhood predominantly populated by older, wealthy residents. When I took Anneka out in her baby carriage, our elderly neighbors appeared especially delighted. We loved Atherton and felt we had finally 'arrived' in Silicon Valley. Yet, the real hard work was still ahead.

Two years after our move to Atherton, Naren's company, Integrated Systems, went public. That was the first time we had actual savings in our bank. We bought our first pet, a puppy for Anneka. Life felt a bit more comfortable in our big home in Atherton. We could also afford to get our house painted now, both inside and outside, paying big bucks—the Atherton rates!

A couple of years later, in 1992, tensions started building in Naren's company between him and the CEO of his acquired company. The CEO probably complained to a board member. We learned that, during the next board meeting, Naren would be asked to step down. I was a board member, so even though I was at full term, with Serena due any day, I wanted to be there. After all, Naren was being thrown out from the very company he had created.

At that meeting, a roundtable discussion took place first. Then all the board members took a vote on whether Naren should stay. Most board members voted in his favor—not just me. Naren was voted in to stay.

I vividly remember that board meeting because my water broke during it. I was sitting in my chair and suddenly felt the seat getting wet. I knew right away what had happened. Nobody in the room knew what to do—men usually don't know what to do when a woman's water breaks. Of course, Naren took me to the hospital for the birth. *Forbes* later published a story about me with the headline 'The Day Vinita Gupta's Water Broke.' I was so embarrassed I wanted to put my head on the table. But I was glad I went to the meeting. I had felt compelled to attend despite being heavily pregnant because of the political battle unfolding over Naren's leadership.

When we looked at our newborn's face, though, we both forgot all our recent worries. We introduced Anneka to her baby sister and involved her in choosing the baby's name. When we brought Serena home, Anneka waited for the day her little sister would be able to sleep in the same room as her. I told her it would be on Christmas Eve. Anneka wanted to do everything for the baby—there was not an ounce of jealousy.

Tragically, while Serena was just a baby, our nanny Julie died prematurely of heart failure. She left a very memorable note for Anneka, which she has kept till date. It was sentimental, to say the least, written to the five-year-old girl she was leaving behind.

Digital Link's Expansion

SUMMIT'S INVESTMENT REQUIRED FORMALIZING OUR board structure. Dick Moore, a senior executive from Hewlett-Packard who had recently completed a startup stint, joined as an outside board member. Summit recommended him, and I soon realized why. Dick brought significant gravitas and statesmanlike experience. He was accomplished, polished, and yet approachable. He became my trusted adviser for the next ten years and made complex business issues easy for me to understand.

I remember telling Dick when I became pregnant with Serena. His response was casual and supportive. It did not affect his view of me—which I was afraid of as a woman business leader. I'd been hesitant to share the news of my first pregnancy with Greg, instead recruiting Naren for it, yet here I was, sitting with Dick and discussing this casually. It highlighted how much I had changed culturally. While I still wore sarees and loved curry, I had grown accustomed to and started appreciating America's less rigid social interactions.

As Digital Link expanded, we required a formal sales structure as well. Curtis, our first hire, had resigned, prompting the need for a more experienced sales executive to build a team. I hired a capable executive, and we systematically established our reseller network, gradually increasing sales volume. Northern Telecom's internal purchases provided steady revenue, consistently buying fifteen to twenty units monthly.

During this time, we expanded beyond our initial T1 modem to more complex, niche products. Our second product took six months to develop, double the time of the first. After Scott, the engineer who proved inadequate, we hired Josh, a brilliant new Stanford graduate with a master's in electrical engineering. Josh designed follow-up products with network management capabilities, demonstrating his understanding of evolving market needs while aligning with our frugal and efficient engineering ethos. He contributed significantly to our growth and success.

By the late 1980s, Digital Link had established itself with our modems and other products, but they were all relatively low-priced items. I knew we couldn't remain a small-dollar product company—we needed to expand our product line to address larger market opportunities and justify our venture funding. Fortunately, the market was shifting dramatically in our favor. The internet was becoming the talk of the town, much like AI is now, in 2025. Money was pouring into internet infrastructure investments; some companies were valued at billions of dollars without even shipping more than a handful of their systems.

Internet traffic was also exploding. Companies like Real.com and Broadcast.com sought to stream video to computers. That would have seemed impossible a decade ago. But in the new era, which promised enormous growth in data usage, there would be an increased need for faster data networks. Our products, though initially designed for voice connections to SL1 PBX systems, used digital technology that positioned us perfectly to capitalize on the emerging data transit markets. In the interconnected world, more data meant more need for high-speed lines—T1 lines. Digital Link's name turned out to be great for marketing our T1 and T3 modems. We decided to boldly expand and build system-level products that were far more complicated and expensive. It was a risky step but one we believed was entirely necessary at the time.

To find what to build next, we started talking to our customers. Our most valuable insights came from customers like WorldCom and British Telecom. They discussed their plans for the internet market with us, revealing the products they would need as this transformation unfolded. Dan Palmer, our VP of engineering, played a key role in these conversations. Salespeople loved bringing him to customer meetings because he could understand their lingo, and if he agreed to design a new product for the customer, he would feel obligated to deliver. This direct customer engagement revealed expanding opportunities. WorldCom told us they planned to upgrade from T1 pipes to T3 pipes, creating an immediate need for T3 versions of our products.

Then they mentioned needing an ATM gateway—an aggregator for managing all this information. ATM (asynchronous transfer mode) was a big thing at that time, representing the future of telecommunications infrastructure. Based on these market signals, we expanded beyond our initial T1 modems. We also developed European equivalents to our domestic products, opening an office in Europe with dedicated marketing and sales staff. By 1993, we had six or seven different products in our portfolio.

The most ambitious addition was the gateway product. This was a huge step up for us, a significant evolution from box-level products to system-level solutions. Instead of a single box that cost a few thousand dollars, the gateway product would cost ten or twenty times as much. It positioned us against established players like Stratacom and Cascade Communications—a different league of competitors. We had to hire a whole suite of software engineers, not just hardware engineers, because the product architecture involved multiple cards communicating across a backplane, with CPU and memory components.

The product expansion fueled the potential for future growth. On top of that, we were coming out extremely profitable. As one of our manufacturing executives observed after joining, 'You have created a money-making machine here, Vinita.' We had 60–70 per cent gross margins on hardware products. That was unheard of, as hardware quickly gets copied, putting pressure on pricing. These incredible margins and revenue growth potential made us attractive for going public at a high valuation. The investment bankers were confident they could find investors interested in buying our shares at the IPO price.

The combination of market momentum, product expansion, and financial performance created perfect conditions for going public. During a board meeting in early 1993, Greg Avis suggested this was a good time to consider IPO. We began interviewing investment banks to get a sense of the appetite for an IPO and what they thought we could price our shares at.

Back then, I still thought of myself, above all, as an engineer. That described my education, my approach to problem-solving, my thinking, and for so many years, my self-conception. But a few years after I founded Digital Link, I finally started to break out of that thinking and came to see myself as a CEO and entrepreneur, a risk-taking change maker. It was exciting and empowering, all building up to February 1994, when I became the first Indian woman to take a tech company public in the United States.

PART IV

GOING PUBLIC

JANUARY 1993 STARTED WITH EXCITING NEWS. PACIFIC Bell announced that it had completed work on the largest Switched Multimegabit Data Service (SMDS) network in the nation, working in partnership with Cisco Systems and my company. Sometimes it's odd, even underwhelming compared to today, to look back on what seemed like an enormous step forward in technology less than forty years ago. But at the time, it was indeed important. Pac Bell had built a network connecting a San Francisco–based computer with more than one hundred links in California and Nevada, operating at a speed of 1.544 megabits per second. For that era, that was very fast! A speed of 5G and those of up to ten gigabits per second were, at that point, unimaginable. 'SMDS is one cornerstone in a broadband superhighway that will eventually reach every one of our customers—residential and business,' Mike Sapien of Pac Bell told the press.

It was a grand adventure, constantly propelling me from one challenge to the next. The pace of Silicon Valley accelerates everything, including your own sense of growth and progress.

It energized me and my team. As the company prospered, I felt a sense of deep satisfaction. To my investors and employees, as we prepared to go public, I was a rock star. It was fun and exhilarating—almost addictive.

I knew it was time to take Digital Link public because the venture capitalists were all sure it was, and it was their job to know. Going public was the only way to generate liquidity for the investors and for me. Dan, our VP of engineering, was going to be my right-hand man on this exciting journey. Greg Avis lined up a bunch of investment bankers to come talk to us. According to Greg, our product area was the hottest telecommunications equipment of the moment, tied as it was to building the booming internet.

In August or September of 1993, we chose to work with both Bear Stearns and a smaller firm, Wessels, Arnold & Henderson, based in Minneapolis. We used Bear Stearns as the lead underwriter. The rule of thumb was that you always wanted to have two investment bankers behind you because it was good for marketing the stock and also for backup, just in case. The analysts from both firms were strong, and Bear Stearns had exceptional marketing machinery for public offerings. The two analysts helped craft the message we would present to investors. I finally got to see how the IPO sausage is really made, and a lot of it is marketing and positioning.

Taking a company public is a grueling ordeal. It is a process. That was true in the 1990s, and I'm sure it's still true now, even if the process has changed somewhat. The investment bankers know which of their customers are interested in technology stocks, and they start with the goal of retaining all those customers. They scout the market and prime their customers for the intended offering. Optimism breeds optimism, and the assumption is that the stock will always take off after you go public and that everyone will immediately make a lot of money.

Then you pay handsomely to have a prospectus written, talking up your potential. This is a very intensive and expensive process. Attorneys from all sides are involved because if you make any exaggerated claims that can't hold up to scrutiny, both the company and the underwriters are liable. This was not an abstract, theoretical risk. The Securities and Exchange Commission (SEC) stood ready to investigate in the event that any company going public made claims that were exaggerated and unsubstantiated.

This was quite different from the way it worked as a private company, when you sought to lure investors by making promising claims. You could basically say anything you wanted because it was assumed that savvy investors would do their due diligence and come to their own conclusions about the merit of the claims you were making. Obviously, every individual investor buying a publicly traded stock cannot take the time to do that kind of due diligence, so the SEC has to protect them. Of course, for me, being honest was easy. It was the only way I knew.

When the attorneys finally presented me with the prospectus that emerged from this elaborate process, I was a little shocked. 'What is this?' I complained. 'You guys have watered it down so much that nobody would want to buy our stock!' I was a new entrepreneur and had never gone public with a company before, but I was confident enough to fight for my company. So, we got to work and hammered out some compromises. As CEO, I had to manage every process, both the ones I knew and the ones I did not. It was a challenge getting that prospectus to a place that satisfied both me and the attorneys.

Next up was the road show, which is when investment bankers take the CEO and management team around the world to pitch to potential investors. We flew all over, giving dog and pony shows to groups of investors in different cities and continents. Then it was back to the airport and on to the next city. London, Paris, New York, Boston—we covered a lot of ground.

I leaned in particular on Jim Marver, a senior managing director of corporate finance for Bear Stearns. He was with me at every stop of the road show and was a fabulous partner. Once again, I was coached on what to say and what not to say. Talking directly to investors, I could overextend a bit, more than we were allowed to say in the prospectus. It was another balancing act, knowing how far to go in describing what we thought we could accomplish.

We started the road show in late 1993, when Anneka was seven and Serena two. It was never easy. For example, we made an IPO presentation to a group of investors in Paris, and then, instead of enjoying a night in Paris, I was in a car to Charles de Gaulle. I took the Concorde home because I wanted to be back the same day. That was the first time I ever flew on a supersonic jet. Paris to JFK Airport is a three-hour flight when you're traveling at twice the speed of sound! I wanted to be home for my young daughters. They missed me, but I missed them too.

You go through a lot of highs during an IPO. You're charged up and think you're invincible. You start thinking differently, faced with this instant success; the psychology of that takes its toll on a lot of people in the Valley. It can totally ruin your head. I had seen Naren go through it—it was not much fun talking to him during that time. So, I tried to stay grounded.

The IPO preparations were intense and all-consuming. We were engineers and salespeople used to selling boxes to telecommunications companies. I had never been taught to sell a story and vision for the future. But in IPOs, investors are buying the vision, not the current company. During mock presentations, my executive team and I initially struggled with this shift. We were all inexperienced and nervous about presenting to institutional investors rather than technical customers. But we all learned on the job, and I gradually realized that different audiences required different strokes.

When I went to Wall Street to sell my stock, people were just flabbergasted. First of all, there were virtually no Indians on Wall Street in those days—no analysts, no venture capitalists, nobody. Only a few Indian-owned companies had gone public, including my husband's company. So, people were just awed by me. But I didn't have time to stop and really take that in. There was no room to feel pompous or proud. You just kept your nose to the ground and worked, worked, worked.

The entire time, we were running on adrenaline. I still had to keep up my regular job of actually running the company. I remember thinking, *I would never have even imagined that this would happen to me.* And I also remember thinking, *I don't want to ever do this again!* While managing this process, we had to maintain daily operations. We had to make sure product development continued moving and sales continued hitting their numbers. This was harder when we spent so much time away and so much time was focused on going public. On top of all of that, I was a mother and a wife—both 24/7 jobs that did not care how busy I was with other things. The demands remained the same.

The S-1 filing for IPO created an unexpected internal challenge at Digital Link. For the first time, employees discovered executive stock holdings when the draft became public domain information. There was significant backlash and resentment when they realized how little they would make compared to me, with my approximately 50 per cent ownership. Some argued that if I was making tens of millions from the IPO, they should be able to make at least half a million. It was difficult to explain that I had taken risks for ten years, starting with nothing, while they had joined later.

This created a challenging dynamic that I had not anticipated. I simply hadn't thought much about equity compensation. Our approach to stock had been influenced by Dick Elkus, an outside adviser, who once said, 'If you treat your stock like dirt, it will be dirt.' Following this philosophy, we treated it like gold and didn't dish out that gold very easily. We ran a disciplined ship regarding equity, but we didn't fully appreciate how this would impact employee sentiment when the company went public.

With the publication of information in the S-1, employees weren't just looking at percentages anymore but actual dollar values. At the projected valuation, my stock was worth approximately $70 million. This seemed astronomical to employees with much smaller stakes. After this backlash, I maybe became a little more liberal with stock distribution, but not dramatically so.

The executive team didn't share the rank-and-file perspective. They understood the typical founder-executive equity split. However, engineers and other staff would compare their grants to offers from other companies without understanding the percentage differences or dilution factors. Someone would complain that at another company they received 100,000 shares, while Digital Link only offered 10,000. They didn't recognize the difference between owning 0.02 per cent of one company versus 1 per cent of another.

These were smart people. Yet, they struggled to make sense of it. This remains a huge problem with tech companies today and a great source of friction. Equity is challenging to get right. We didn't get it right. But I don't know many who get it perfect either. We started losing some employees in the run-up to the IPO as competitors came and offered them bigger packages. That would become an even bigger problem after the IPO, when the markets turned.

In January 1994, approximately nine years after founding Digital Link, we completed our initial public offering at around $13 per share. The stock subsequently rose to $25, creating substantial paper wealth. My shares alone were worth approximately $74 million. That was a huge amount of money at that time. I felt some relief, but I also knew I was not finished yet. I wanted to grow Digital Link into something hugely successful. It's why I got into the game. The money was nice, but I was there to build a company, not sit on a cruise ship and count my cash.

IPOs are famously all about timing, and it looked like our timing was good. In early 1994, we were right at the cusp of the internet changing the world of business. Investors were eager to position themselves to take advantage. They were also eager to understand this rapidly evolving digital space. So our story resonated well with everybody; it was not a hard sell.

Days after we went public, the federal reserve announced its first interest rate hike in five years. The IPO market collapsed as a result, meaning that any company trying to go public was stymied. One venture capitalist told me, 'You got out of the chute just in time!' This was another lesson I learned: Not everything is under our control. The timing here worked out for us, but it didn't for many others.

Support System

THROUGHOUT THE CHALLENGES OF LEADING A PUBLIC company while raising young children, I relied on an invisible support system that made my dual roles possible. This network of caregivers and household help rarely appears in business narratives, but it proved absolutely essential in my ability to function as CEO during this demanding period.

Julie was our first nanny. She wasn't just an employee—she became part of our family, staying with us for six years. When Digital Link went public in January 1994, I shared this success with Julie by giving her shares of company stock, which she later gave to her nephew. This acknowledgment felt important; her contribution had made my professional achievement possible.

When Julie passed away, I was totally devastated. I knew nothing about what my kids ate or how to take care of them, and I still had a company to run. I again tapped on Mothers in Need. They first provided temporary help, and later on, Ginger joined our family.

Ginger had raised two daughters of her own, and she cared for my girls for the next twelve years. Ginger was loving, conscientious, and vigilant—she once scolded a kindergarten teacher for forgetting to put my daughter's sweater on. Her presence provided stability during the most turbulent period of Digital Link's history, including the gateway product challenges and Naren's health crisis, which I'll speak of soon.

Four years into working for us, Ginger gave notice, saying she needed weekends off after working long hours during the week. This potential change created anxiety throughout the family. When eleven-year-old Anneka noticed a new candidate visiting, she insisted on meeting whomever I might select for a full-time nanny. I suggested we might find someone who didn't discipline them so much, but Serena shot back, 'I love Ginger, Mommy!' Serena was the one who used to push back on Ginger, so this made me realize that I wasn't fully aware of the girls' relationship with Ginger.

At my husband's urging, I went to Ginger's cottage and asked, 'Would you reconsider staying on?' We both had tears in our eyes when she agreed. This emotional moment revealed something important: Ginger was as attached to my daughters as they were to her. What I had viewed primarily as employment was, for Ginger, a deep personal connection. Taking care of my daughters wasn't just a job for her.

Beyond childcare, I relied on a house manager. Gladys provided crucial household support that kept our family functioning during the most intense periods of company and personal crisis. These relationships were never merely transactional, though. In the hustle of managing a public company during challenging times, I sometimes treated them with the same strict and demanding approach I used with company executives. In hindsight, I recognize I could have been kinder and gentler, though I was always generous with praise when warranted.

Almost every founder who gets close to an IPO has a support system like this. Most do not talk about it. They should. Taking a company public and raising a family without help is not really possible. I am grateful that my support network was there for me along the way and that they remain with me even long after this period.

Public Pressure

THE SHIFT FROM PRIVATE TO PUBLIC COMPANY REALLY changed my job as CEO. At Digital Link, I'd always focused on building a lasting business. And that was still my game plan. I had outside investors who trusted my IPO story. I wasn't about to disappoint them.

But the public market created mental pressures I hadn't expected. Every morning there was a report card showing the stock price. That was grueling until I got used to it. Though I didn't obsessively check our share price each morning, news inevitably found me. If the stock went up, I heard about it even if I didn't want to. Somebody would come and tell me, 'Did you see what happened to the stock today?' When our stock climbed, excitement permeated the office. When it dropped, tensions rose and questions followed. The volatility wasn't just financial; it was emotional and cultural.

The public market's constant judgment created emotional ups and downs that clouded decision-making if not handled carefully. Learning to create mental distance from stock movements and analyst opinions became as important as technical or business know-how. Leaders who get too emotionally tied to market opinions lose perspective right when clear thinking is needed most.

Building a healthy company culture proved equally important to combat this pressure. As an immigrant woman who had overcome large obstacles through determination and hard work, I had developed habits that worked well during our startup days but, in its expanded form, were now unhealthy. The pressure I felt as CEO flowed down to every executive and eventually to all the employees. When I worked in unhealthy ways, I silently encouraged similar behavior throughout Digital Link.

It was board members such as Dick Moore and Dick Alberding, men with much experience running large public companies, who taught me to balance my commitments with my well-being. One key insight I learned was that working myself to the point of collapse didn't help the company. True leadership meant making sure I could keep leading, not harming my health for short-term gains. It was particularly after my family's health crisis that I made an effort to show more balanced approaches, leaving at reasonable hours when possible, openly talking about family commitments, and admitting my own limits when appropriate. These small changes gradually influenced the company culture.

The board members provided vital support in developing this more open company culture. Dick Moore's steady interest in my family and personal well-being showed that these matters were not only appropriate but actually belonged in business discussions. Dick Alberding's invitations to his home with his wife Marilyn showed that business relationships could include real human connection. I didn't realize then that other CEOs didn't usually have supportive boards that also challenged them when necessary. These interactions slowly changed how I thought about professional boundaries, and helped bring personal well-being into my leadership approach.

Going public also changed the board dynamics at Digital Link. Meetings now included lengthy discussions about investor relations, disclosure requirements, and market perception—topics that had barely registered when we were private. The focus sometimes shifted from building the best products to meeting quarterly expectations and how to position the company for the quarterly earnings calls.

Ten months after the IPO, I promoted Dan, our VP of engineering, to be the president of the company—hoping he would become the CEO one day. However, soon after the promotion, Dan shared that the engineers were having technical difficulties with the gateway product. Our ambitious gateway product—the system-level solution priced at $100,000—became our biggest technical and professional challenge. The complexity of integrating multiple cards and sophisticated software proved more difficult than anticipated. The specific problems weren't apparent during component development, instead emerging during system integration.

Three months later, in mid-1995, he was able to assess how much longer the product would take to be released to the general market. The product was already in the hands of one customer, so I still had high hopes.

But the gateway product delay meant revenues wouldn't come in as predicted. This forced us to adjust market expectations. Wall Street analysts had created a story about Digital Link starting to sell this gateway, and when we pushed back the timeline, they knew how to smell problems. The disclosure rules at that time were different—we never gave numbers, so it was more gamesmanship. But the specific technical challenges with our gateway product exemplified how public markets struggle with typical engineering realities.

I leaned on our investment bankers for guidance on communicating with Wall Street. One piece of advice stuck with me: 'It's not what you say; it's the tone of your voice that counts.' In my inexperience, I interpreted this as needing to talk up your stock, when they were actually advising me to deliver information with confidence and matter-of-factness.

When we announced the delay of the gateway product, our stock tumbled. Within a few months after that, I was under enormous pressure to let Dan go. I knew Dan better. Engineering delays are not unusual. But post-IPO, when Dick Alberding, a superior to Dick Moor at HP, joined our board, he'd questioned my decision to promote Dan. Now, he asked, 'Why is Dan still here?' Ultimately, I did let Dan go in mid-1995. That broke my heart. But in business you seek advice and listen to a more experienced board.

Through all these challenges, leadership took on a new meaning for me. I had to discover when to listen and when to lead. This is why no one can ever learn leadership in a classroom. Only real-life experiences can teach you what to do.

Dan's dismissal was not the only fallout from the product delay. The very next day after the announcement, a lawsuit was filed claiming that management had misled investors about product readiness and revenue projections. When developing complex technology products, the projections of timing are, at best, an estimate. We were not misleading anyone. This reality was well understood by technology investors. The allegations were painful given how hard we'd worked to build honest relationships with customers and investors. It was humiliating to be sued and labeled as liars.

The lawsuit was filed by Bill Lerach's San Diego–based firm, which had the reputation for being corporate ambulance chasers. This lawsuit finally got settled four years later, along with another lawsuit during our reverse IPO stage.

Psychologically I was being challenged—public market optics, product delays, Dan's departure, employee retention issues due to stock price decline, and now a lawsuit. I made the decision: 'I will hire someone to replace me as CEO.' The board agreed. Through Heidrick & Struggles search firm, we found Jack. He came from Northern Telecom, Canada and had a finance background rather than a technical one. He was an executive with wide operating experience and a cheerful demeanor.

Jack joined Digital Link in mid-1996 as its new CEO. Employees were excited when I introduced him, which led me to believe I'd made the right choice. I was hopeful that with this change, he would instill a healthy company culture. I couldn't have known that things were only about to get more complicated.

The Heart Attack

ON VALENTINE'S DAY, 1997, THE IDEA OF A SUPPORT network took on a darker meaning for me and my family. We went from receiving support from our nannies to Naren requiring literal life support in the hospital.

Naren and I were packing for a ski vacation with our family and friends. We were walking up and down the stairs, getting skis and packing bags, when he said that he had a pain in his back and wanted to lie down. At first, I thought nothing of it. I continued packing. I only started to grow concerned when he asked me to bring him a book from downstairs about heart health. He wanted to consult the book to see if he was exhibiting symptoms of a heart attack. He didn't tell me that, of course, but he didn't need to. I knew, and my heart sank.

When he called the Palo Alto Medical Foundation to speak with a doctor on call, I began to really worry. I watched him walking back and forth while speaking on the phone, describing his symptoms. He'd read through the chapters, but there was little mention of upper back pain. At that time, there was more focus on chest pain. (Today, we all know better.) He then continued to lay there quietly, and I continued packing, now with a cloud of worry in the front of my mind.

A little while later, he said, 'Let's go to the hospital.' Knowing him, the request was extraordinary. Naren's serious expression got me really worried now. Of course, I dropped everything and pulled the car out, then walked in front of him down the stairs while calling Ginger, who lived on the premises, leaving her in charge of the kids for God knew how long.

On that day, our lives changed forever.

Naren had always been active. He loved hiking, skiing, swimming—anything outdoors. He played racquetball two times a week for fun and exercise. Yes, he was not as thin as he had been when we were married, but he was not markedly heavy either. We ate fairly healthy, avoiding junk food and not consuming a lot of meat. But he did enjoy going to restaurants and overate—in my opinion.

Naren also came from a family with a troubling legacy of heart problems. His relatives tended to die at a relatively young age from cardiac issues. We knew this, but somehow we didn't believe his biological predisposition would affect us. His mother had died at just fifty-seven years old, an unusually early age for a woman to succumb to heart disease. This happened while she was living with us temporarily after his parents' retirement. I was just thirty years old when I had to rush her to the same Stanford Hospital.

His grandparents had also died young. 'It runs in the family,' people would say, but in India at that time, there wasn't the same awareness or detailed medical tracking of such hereditary conditions. People just accepted death at a younger age as part of their reality. Medical care was also not as advanced. Yes, some of the most advanced hospitals in India in the late 1990s could provide care on par with the West, but there was far less access to cutting-edge healthcare.

The first real indication of this family vulnerability came when Naren's brother, who was only about two years older than him, suffered a devastating stroke at just at the age of forty-five. It was shocking—a man in his prime, otherwise seemingly normal, suddenly struck down. His condition was so severe that his wife brought him to America, hoping that the advanced medical care here might offer some solution that wasn't available in India.

We arranged for his brother to be evaluated at Stanford, where the prognosis was grim. The doctors determined that his heart was enlarged, and the stroke had caused catastrophic brain damage. His intelligence, they told us, had been reduced to that of a two-year-old. His wife was heartbroken. Like many people from abroad, she had believed America was a 'miraculous place' where her husband would be 'fixed.' Instead, we all faced the harsh reality that his brain damage was permanent.

He and his wife stayed with us for a month and a half. Neither of them had ever left India before, and his wife didn't speak a word of English. They were completely dependent on us, particularly me, for everything from communication to transportation to emotional support. Eventually, they returned to India, where he lived for a few more years with the help of caregivers, before passing away.

This family tragedy occurred about five or six years before Naren's own heart attack. It should have been a warning, a glimpse into the genetic vulnerability that might also affect my husband. But Naren was only forty-eight, seemingly aware and healthy. We were both young CEOs, in the thick of the battle to grow our companies. We had two young daughters, and our lives revolved around family and friends. We had very full lives. We simply didn't think anything could happen to him.

We were wrong.

Stanford Hospital was just ten minutes away. Halfway there, at the intersection where we would turn onto the road that led to the Stanford Emergency Room, he said, 'I think you need to call an ambulance.'

This really frightened me. Had his brain already been affected by whatever was happening? 'I'm driving,' I replied, my heartbeat accelerating. 'The hospital is five minutes away.'

It was nearly midnight when we arrived at the emergency room. Because of his chest and back pain, they took him in immediately while I parked the car. By the time I joined him, they were already running blood tests and had him hooked up to an EKG monitor. The doctors kept asking if he was on drugs—a seemingly odd question for a professional, healthy-looking forty-eight-year-old man. I later found out that when someone his age came in with atypical symptoms, this was the standard question. The pain in his back, rather than chest, wasn't the classic heart attack symptom they were trained to recognize, though research has since shown this presentation is actually quite common.

When the blood test results came back, the doctor noted that Naren's enzyme levels, indicating muscle damage, were very high, but they warned it was nonspecific, meaning it might not be heart related. They asked if he had a cardiologist.

'No,' he answered. 'I've never seen a cardiologist.'

We were told to wait for the on-call cardiologist from Palo Alto Medical Foundation, who had been summoned. An hour and a half later, Dr. Mullin arrived, looked at the test results, and returned with the news that would change everything: 'Mr. Gupta, you are undergoing a major heart attack right now.'

Standing next to his bed, I was frightened. Life was changing in front of my eyes. I did not know if he would live or die within minutes. I did not even understand what a heart attack was. All I knew was that people died of heart attacks.

Medical terminologies were getting tossed at us left and right. Dr. Mullin said, 'Let me get the team ready for angiogram and angioplasty.'

Naren asked, 'How many such surgeries have you performed?'

The doctor hurriedly said, 'I will answer all your questions, but first let me get the OR team ready.'

The urgency was evident as the doctor himself wheeled Naren's hospital bed toward the operating room. I waited outside, wondering if my husband would emerge alive.

Thankfully, the procedure—an angioplasty to unblock his clogged artery—was successful. They used a balloon to open the blocked artery, though no stent was placed. Naren wouldn't receive a stent until 2020, managing somehow for twenty-three years without one. But the news following the surgery was devastating. Naren's ejection fraction—a measure of how efficiently his heart was pumping blood—was just 30 per cent, far below the 70–80 per cent of a healthy person.

'What does that mean?' I asked Dr. Mullin.

'It probably means he may not be able to walk,' he responded. 'He may be wheelchair bound.'

I was speechless. Naren loved the outdoors. He had boundless energy. We loved traveling. I could not imagine him confined to a wheelchair. It would be very hard for him, the kids, and me.

The doctor further informed us that Naren's five-year survival chances were not promising due to the severity of his cardiac event.

Five years, I thought. *That's not very long.* Would my husband, the man I had built my life with, the man whom I depended on as a partner and confidant, only live into his early fifties? This did not seem possible. The prognosis hung over us like a shadow for years, though, thankfully, Naren would prove it all wrong.

Almost immediately, Naren began to defy these pessimistic prognoses. Despite the low ejection fraction, he was able to walk soon after being discharged. He gradually regained strength, and his energy never seemed diminished beyond a bit of fatigue. We immediately implemented radical lifestyle changes: the Ornish vegetarian diet, substituting olive oil for all other fats, eliminating sweets (which Naren loved), and implementing a daily twenty-minute walk regimen instead of his weekly racquetball game. We became extreme in our dietary discipline, recognizing that his life literally depended on it. I even cut back my own sweet consumption to one day a week, though I loved desserts almost as much as he did.

The heart attack had a huge impact on me. I had a company that I was trying to grow, on the height of an IPO. I had employees to manage. I had two young daughters who needed our attention, care and love. I had an extended family that we frequently supported. And now I had a far more important mission: keep my husband alive and return him to good health. I didn't speak of it at the time, but it was overwhelming. I never could have imagined so much on my shoulders. I started to worry for my own health, which, thankfully, remained strong. But life is never easy, so I didn't even really stop to think. I just kept pushing forward.

Unfortunately, we had little time to fully process the implications of the heart attack before another health crisis emerged. Naren developed ulcerative colitis, a gastrointestinal condition that causes inflammation and bleeding in the digestive tract. This is not an uncommon development after a cardiac event. The body's systems are all interconnected, and the stress and medications following a heart attack can trigger other conditions. The illness meant he was constantly bleeding and very weak, with lower energy. I was totally stressed out. He never asked for sympathy, but he was clearly not himself.

Despite this new diagnosis, in June 1997, Naren insisted on traveling to India to receive a distinguished alumni award from IIT New Delhi. He really, really wanted to go. IIT had been an important chapter in his life. The bleeding had already started, but the honor meant so much to him that we decided to make the journey. With my better judgment, we left our two young daughters at home with Ginger. It was the only trip we ever took without them.

On our return journey, while stopping at Hong Kong, the bleeding became so severe that Naren said, 'I think I need to go to the hospital.' We asked the airline to unload our bags and quickly deboarded. But I had no idea how to take him to a hospital, or even which one. This was before cell phones and internet. Thankfully, the airline helped with the arrangements, and we arrived at the community hospital. Naren was placed in a ward with hundreds of patients, a far cry from the halls of Stanford Hospital. The hospital staff barely spoke English and were not very communicative.

For a week, I was stranded in Hong Kong with my seriously ill husband. Each day, I spoke with his brother Ash in New York and our physician back home, Dr. Croke, trying to determine the best course of action. Eventually, Ash and I decided that Naren needed to be transported back to the United States. Dr. Croke arranged for a team from Stanford—a physician and a nurse—to fly to Hong Kong and accompany Naren on a business class flight back to San Francisco. He was taken directly from the airport to Stanford Hospital, where he would spend the next four weeks.

Even at Stanford, the bleeding from the ulcerative colitis wouldn't stop, and the doctors were considering removing parts of his intestines as a last resort. This was a major surgery, not to mention the lifestyle impact it would have on his health and ability to digest food.

In a miraculous turn of events, an Indian friend who was a pathologist visited Naren in the hospital. He looked at Naren's pathology report and thought he saw a virus that might be causing further inflammation and bleeding. I shared that with Dr. Croke, who got an infectious disease expert involved. Soon, this expert started Naren on medication to combat the virus, which he said could take three weeks to take effect. Ultimately, it proved successful. His intestines remained intact, though he lost forty pounds during this ordeal.

When he finally came home around September 1997, he was in a wheelchair, severely weakened by the consecutive health crises. What had begun as a heart attack in February had evolved into a six-month medical nightmare. It was very rocky for me and the girls, to put it mildly.

Throughout these harrowing months, our daughters—barely five and nine at the time—knew something was terribly wrong. But they couldn't fully comprehend the gravity of the situation. The emotional impact became clear one day when I returned home to find my older daughter upset. 'Saima said Dad is going to die,' she told me, referring to the daughter of one of our family friends. How does one explain such adult fears to a child? How do you reassure them when you yourself are terrified?

During Naren's hospital stays, I would sit with the children and pray—something I did in times of crisis. 'Please, God, give me the strength to pull me out of this,' I would say in English so the children could understand. It felt as though everything in our lives were falling apart.

Slowly, Naren started recovering. I was taking on more responsibilities with the children, both physically and emotionally. I was the one to carry our sleeping five-year-old up the stairs after evenings out, never expecting Naren to manage such a task with his weakened heart, even when he protested. For years after, I shouldered not just the physical burden but the emotional weight of maintaining stability for two small children whose world had been upended. There was no other option. We had to keep Naren alive and healthy. There was a strong possibility he would never return to his original level of health and activity, but you cannot choose such things in life. You can only work through them and do your best.

All of this was happening against the backdrop of continued professional challenges in Naren's company and Digital Link. By 1997—before his heart attack—Naren was no longer the CEO. Having won the battle in 1992 to stay on, he faced several senior executives' resignations. He brought in David St. Charles as the CEO but remained chairman, going to work every day. Even in this reduced role, Naren was watching like a hawk. The company was his baby. He was always in 'founder mode,' as they say today.

After the heart attack and ulcerative colitis crisis, I made Naren promise not to return to work daily anymore. He fully handed over all oversight, remaining chairman of the board.

The shadow of mortality never fully lifted from our lives after his heart attack. Even as he recovered and years passed, I lived on pins and needles, especially when his adventurous spirit reasserted itself. When he decided, years later, to trek to Ama Dablam Base Camp in Nepal at fourteen thousand feet despite his compromised heart, I was beside myself with worry. 'A guy with a 30 per cent ejection fraction wants to go to fourteen thousand feet,' I said with exasperation. 'If you die there, you are on your own.'

Of course, I did not mean that, but we never minced words with each other. And, truthfully, I couldn't comprehend why he would take such risks given his condition. But his determination to live life fully never waned.

The only consistent concession he made to his condition was wearing a life vest when we went snorkeling on vacations. Otherwise, he continued to push boundaries, and I continued to worry. Every trip, every exertion, every minor complaint of discomfort triggered my anxiety about losing him. Many times during our travels, while others in our group would go on excursions, I would stay behind with Naren when he mentioned chest discomfort or other concerning symptoms.

The doctors had given him five years. Thanks to our lifestyle changes, excellent medical care, and perhaps sheer determination, he lived for more than twenty years beyond that prognosis. But those extra years came with a constant undercurrent of anxiety—for me, if not for him. His heart attack became the dividing line in our lives: everything that came before, and everything that came after.

Looking back on that period from before and after February 1997, I see it as an arc of transformation—from the high-flying tech entrepreneurs we had been to more grounded individuals with a profound awareness of life's fragility. The heart attack that should have killed Naren instead changed him, changed me, changed our marriage, and changed our approach to life itself. It gave us a deeper appreciation for simple pleasures. It forced us to confront our limitations and accept help when our natural inclination was to be the helpers. It humbled us in ways that business setbacks never could.

Perhaps most significantly, it revealed the true foundation of our partnership. When stripped of the trappings of professional success and the distractions of daily ambition, what remained was a commitment to face whatever came next.

Digital Decline

IN LATE 1997, I RETURNED TO WORK (FULL-TIME) AFTER attending to Naren's health crises. Digital Link's revenue growth hadn't picked up, and Jack was still an unproven CEO in a small company setup. Upon my return, my longtime trusted CFO privately shared with me how compensation for the salespeople had been changed. Jack had immediately begun tinkering with the compensation, believing the salespeople were not properly motivated due to the current setup.

His changes made things worse. The sales team had been operating under a system the previous VPs of sales had carefully developed. In that system, a salesperson was strictly compensated only for sales in their territory, which is very traditional in the industry. Jack's new system was based on the goal of developing a market for our network management products. It left the sales team confused. They literally did not know what they were getting paid for. Plus, the newer products were harder to sell, and the sales team was struggling.

Jack did not prove to be the 'nuts and bolts' guy, important for smaller, dynamic companies like ours. Within a few weeks after my return, in early 1998, Jack told me he had been recruited by the famous venture capitalist John Doerr for another startup and couldn't turn that down. While I hadn't been particularly happy with his performance, his departure now left me battling a lot of problems and forced me to figure out how to do everything myself. The outside CEO experiment had failed, causing us to lose valuable time and sales talent during a critical period.

I returned to my CEO role. My first act was to find a new VP of engineering. I hired a woman named Lana, who was born and raised in Russia. She came from Sprint and Intel. She knew telecommunications and was very smart. I found her through Heidrick & Struggles, who gave me one pro bono executive hire since Jack had left so quickly. That was the Silicon Valley support system at work again. I was looking for someone to duplicate Dan Palmer—someone who could motivate an engineering team and see the future in products but was also not afraid to go in front of customers.

Culturally, Lana was very different from the executives I'd had before. She was a tough and hard-driving person, which is what I wanted. She worked hard to deliver the new promised products, but recruiting good engineers was a struggle for the company, especially in an overheated market. She recommended her husband's consulting company to get the work done. I agreed and approved it. However, consultants are much more expensive than employees, and this approach is not sustainable over the long term.

Our original CFO had become disenchanted with Jack and resigned, and I now had to search for someone to fill that role. I hired Naresh Kapahi. He was a good friend of Naren and I, and he was an experienced CFO in private companies, a good manager of people, and a good negotiator. His skills came handy in our next phase of the company.

Over time, bit by bit, the investment analysts stopped covering us. We became out of sight and out of mind to investors. Our stock started to slide. We were no longer the darling newcomers. There were other, more promising telecom companies building newer technologies. While we were solidly profitable, we were not living up to our growth promise. Our 25 per cent growth rate was good enough to go public, but without the gateway product, our story was not nearly as compelling.

Digital Link was also considered an out-of-favor public company. The internet market had gotten overheated. New dot-coms were going public. Light was shining on them instead of companies like ours, which had gone public at the dawn of the internet.

Now, when employees saw our share price decline, many questioned their future with Digital Link. We had lost stature in the minds of our engineers. We were now viewed as a legacy provider even though we were only a few years old. Our products were not 'sexy' anymore—even our gateway was viewed as behind the times compared to bigger stories painted by newer startups. It's very difficult to keep an engineer in a company whose stock is not doing well, especially when the market is hot. Each engineering departure created a cascade of problems. With a complex product like the gateway system, losing key technical talent slowed development further, creating a self-fulfilling prophecy.

The old executive team, responsible for our success and IPO, had already been dismantled. Some were let go by me, some left under Jack, and the VP of manufacturing had passed away. I readily took responsibility for the problems at Digital Link—after all, the buck stopped with me. But the market had changed too.

I was growing and learning from the new leadership challenges that came with the territory, but it was hard going. I also got hardened. More and more, I felt that going public had fundamentally changed our company dynamics in subtle but important ways. The constant external judgment created pressures that affected every decision, from product development timelines to executive hiring. The scrutiny magnified normal business challenges, turning them into potential crises. We had taken a major turn for the worse.

Reverse IPO

FIVE YEARS INTO OUR IPO, BY 1999, THE PUBLIC MARKET journey had become increasingly difficult for Digital Link. It was affecting everything from employee morale to customer confidence. The gateway product had indeed shipped, contrary to what skeptics believed possible, but it wasn't working well enough to generate the projected revenues that had fueled our successful public offering.

Seeing my struggles with Digital Link, one day Naren said, 'Why not reprivatize the company, fix the product direction, give out cheap employee stock options, and take it public again?'

I immediately pushed back. 'It is a huge financial risk. I don't think so!' I was also worried about reputational risk if I failed. I was one of the few female immigrant CEOs in Silicon Valley and the only Indian woman ever to offer an IPO on the Nasdaq. The IPO represented not just business success, but also personal validation.

But Naren had a habit of being persistent. In the next board meeting, he floated the idea of reprivatization—or a reverse takeover. Dick Alberding, drawing on his decades of Hewlett-Packard experience, liked it a lot. Digital Link's fundamental business remained sound despite our stock performance. 'You're still generating positive cash flow from operations, and your core products are profitable,' he observed. Because we had not shipped the gateway product on time, the market hurt our price. So, we believed the market simply wasn't paying attention to our underlying value.

This was a revolutionary idea, as I could gauge from the other board members' reactions. But they were listening. Once private, we could operate in stealth mode and get moving in the right direction. The board members were calming down and even getting enthusiastic as the discussions proceeded. Later that night, Naren said, 'The company has enough cash to repurchase public shares, while the profits would pay for running it until we're ready to take it public again.' At the time, the internet market was still very strong. But I was still not fully convinced.

Naren and I, as a couple, had taken big financial risks by starting two companies in the same household. We had put all our savings into our businesses and hadn't drawn salaries for a number of years, running our home on a meager income. Naren's company went through its own ups and downs, and now it was my turn to ride the rollercoaster. We stuck it out. Naren was steadfast in his belief: 'No risk, no reward.' The privatization of Digital Link was another huge step in that direction.

Slowly but surely, he converted me, even though I dragged my feet. Eventually, I thought to myself, *Why not?* I was even getting excited at the idea of reprivatization. Its newness and creativity were appealing. It was an unusual tactic, for sure. Virtually no tech companies did it. In fact, when taking the company public, there were hundreds of attorneys available, as they knew how lucrative it would be for them. But few ever took one private, or wanted to.

With great difficulty, I found an attorney, a senior partner at the law firm Latham & Watkins. Kit was a tenacious and creative thinker, just like Naren, and fortunately, he was able to guide us through the process. He remains a friend to this day.

At the next board meeting in mid-1999, I presented a preliminary privatization process and plan, with Kit's coaching. With my ownership well above 50 per cent, the risk was entirely ours; we would buy back the stock from the outside shareholders. The board discussion helped me get their insights, and their acceptance, which I valued. They understood the frustration with how the market undervalued profitable technology companies in favor of unprofitable 'story stocks' during the emerging internet boom. It was a new experiment for them and us. In running a company, you are responsible for the successes and the failures.

The process required us to have two attorneys—one for the buyer and one for the seller. Kit represented Naren and me (the buyers), and the board (the sellers) used the company attorney to represent public shareholders. This arrangement increased the legal costs of privatization. That said, the real cost to Naren and me was when we accepted a higher buyback price in negotiations with the board on the advice of their attorney. Naren and I later learned that we ended up paying $2 per share more than we had to. In addition, the buyback news leaked ahead of the announcement, so the market price of shares rose. We had to increase our price further because we could not buy back below the public market price. We had to pay a premium for our control. This is very normal for management buybacks, which is what it was. Those were the expensive buyback and privatization lessons we had to learn.

In June 1999, right after we publicly announced the formation of the special committee to evaluate privatization, Bill Lerach's law firm filed its second lawsuit against Digital Link.

This new legal action claimed we were cheating shareholders by taking the company private at an unfair low valuation. The suit argued that as majority shareholder, I was abusing my position to acquire Digital Link at a discount. The speed of this filing was remarkable—suggesting they maintained template complaints ready to deploy against any privatization announcement.

Lerach's firm was aggressive. They filed lawsuits based on little information and then used discovery processes to develop more specific allegations. All they had to do was quickly find one shareholder of Digital Link shares and file a class action suit on his or her behalf. For companies already navigating difficult market conditions, these lawsuits, although frivolous, sucked up a CEO's attention and time.

The deposition took place in Latham & Watkins's offices in Menlo Park. With two sets of attorneys from each side, it was an interesting scene. Here, I saw how the actual legal battle between attorneys takes place. Lerach's side had one set of lawyers representing 'misleading the investors' lawsuit and another for 'not paying fair market price' for the shares being repurchased. Kit's litigation lawyer coached me on how to answer. He said the answers should be 'Yes,' 'No,' or 'I don't remember.' Specifically, they told me that when asked if I were paying the maximum fair price to shareholders, I should just say, 'We are paying the fair market price.' 'Maximum' was their trap word. My attorneys also negotiated a maximum of three hours of deposition time for me. My other attorney was from Wilson Sonsini, the most reputable tech law firm in business at the time.

Lerach's firm's business model aimed for settlement rather than trial. Settlements usually came from DNO (directors and officers) liability insurance that the companies carried, with coverage running in the millions of dollars. This approach reflected a strategic calculation that most companies (and their insurers) would pay settlements rather than endure years of expensive litigation, regardless of whether the lawsuit had merit.

Our polished Silicon Valley attorneys were skillful negotiators. They rightly sensed that Lerach's attorneys would like to settle before the reprivatization date (published on the buyback offer to the shareholders). Otherwise they had no case, as we wouldn't have the DNO insurance as a private company. When, in the deposition, the prosecution came empty-handed, both lawsuits got settled in a hurry, within the DNO insurance amount.

Market Dizziness and Letting Go

THE MARKET REMAINED OVERHEATED. HIRING WAS tough—unlike when we first got VC funding, when we were considered a company in hot space. In the midst of this rough climate, I had to fill a VP of sales spot. I first hired a VP who lived in Florida, as it was difficult to attract senior executives from the Valley. This guy was supposed to be interim, but I had to let him go quickly. He was padding his expense reports. This was a problem I never encountered with my previous executive team or anyone else in Silicon Valley, and I was shocked.

Shortly thereafter, I hired Sherm Silverman from Seagate, the disk drive company. He was tenacious and drove hard bargains. At the time of the interview, he stated, 'I will join your company if you give me the opportunity to head both sales and marketing.' This wasn't unreasonable for high-powered salespeople. I told him, 'Let me think about the marketing part.' He accepted.

His transition into the company was a bit rocky. Sherm was demanding of his salespeople. He would say, 'Set me five customer calls—I'm coming to Dallas.' He did not use the carrot-and-stick approach like a good VP of sales. It's okay to be tough, but you also have to earn respect first. Sherm came from a different company culture, more cutthroat. Good long-term salespeople did not like that, but I called it change.

He also did things that I found comical. I remember driving with him to the airport. He was sitting with his foot high up on the dashboard, looking for a parking spot. When he saw someone he thought was pulling out of their space, Sherm rolled down the window and asked with a smile, 'Are you leaving?'

The person said, 'No, I was just repositioning the car.'

Sherm shot back, 'Is your spot for sale?'

That's how aggressive he could be. I liked his toughness and creativity, which was much needed, as we had become too relaxed as an organization.

A couple of months later, Sherm asked me for a meeting. I had suspected he wanted a discussion about giving him control of marketing. He came to me with a drop of blood oozing from his chin. I wondered if he knew it was there. I mean, who shows up for a meeting with their boss with blood on their face? But by now I had learned to expect the unexpected. I tried not to get too distracted.

Sherm suggested that if he were running both sales and marketing, it would be better for the company because he would have more control. But he also quickly backpedaled, saying he had understood that it was not a promise but a consideration for the future. That was a relief.

At that point, he took out a tissue, wiped the blood from his chin with a laugh, and said, 'Vinita, I was just negotiating.' With a smile, he said, 'I once used this blood-on-the-face technique to get sympathy when asking a customer for a large order.' For me, it was an interesting sales technique. I smiled to myself, and told Naren the story at home over dinner.

In mid-2000, just eight months after we had taken Digital Link private, the other shoe dropped. WorldCom, our biggest customer, called to cancel all their orders on our books. When I hung up the phone, my first thought was damage control. *What is the short-term cash impact?*

I also worried about the impact on our inventory. *How much inventory will we get stuck with?* We typically kept ninety days of inventory to ship orders in a timely fashion; I didn't want to miss shipments to customers. Now that inventory was enough for six to eight months.

With the WorldCom troubles already made public, they did not place more orders. We soon flipped from being profitable to losing money. And it wasn't just WorldCom—other ISP customers also reduced their orders, and everything slowed down. With reduced revenues and no signs of a market turnaround, I had to turn my attention to making cuts. Unfortunately, I did multiple layoffs, hoping things would start coming back up. Each one was painful for me and the organization.

I remember standing with tears in my eyes as employees packed their belongings and vacated their offices. Each step seemed harder than the previous one. Nothing was hidden from the employees—they all knew the situation—but that didn't make it easier on anyone. I should have done the layoffs in one shot. I wish I had learned that sooner. The steady drip of layoffs only created more pain.

It was also a tough market, and Sherm couldn't turn around our sales trends. More than that, other executives did not gel well with Sherm. He was a 'character'—like many of my early employees. I finally had to ask him to resign. Most surprisingly, he was the only executive who had tears in his eyes when I fired him. He said, 'I am sorry. I disappointed you.' He meant it.

Then I had to let Lana go to save money—the company needed to get things done with less. Lana and I remained friends, and I really liked her as a person, but neither I nor the engineers in the company considered it healthy to have half of the engineering team be a consulting company run by the husband of our CTO. As a startup CEO, I was yet to learn to draw these boundaries.

Even though we were impacted early on, it was the beginning of a steep slide in the market. By early April 2001, the Nasdaq had already dropped by over 25 per cent from its peak a year ago. IPO investors were now valuing companies with profitability as opposed to those with hyper growth and the promise of future profits.

The Valley had changed overnight. Employees, founders, and investment bankers were all on an unsustainable path. It was dizzying, watching the landscape change. Telecom industry giants like Lucent, Cisco, and Alcatel crashed hard. Even the sexy telecom startups, like JDS Uniphase, hit a wall. Every stock related to the internet or technology was in free fall. Even my very first customer and previous employer, Northern Telecom, had to file for Chapter 11. WorldCom filed for bankruptcy in 2002. Its CEO, Bernie Ebber, went to jail for borrowing money from the company and for fraudulent accounting practices—for which his CFO blamed him.

The environment in Silicon Valley was dark. Digital Link's engineering director of the gateway product, who had left, told me he became a day trader and lost all his savings. One of Naren's analyst at Hambrecht & Quist committed suicide, and the founder and CEO of one of my competitors died (rumor was from a heart attack) one month after his company filed for bankruptcy. He was almost fifty. I myself had young kids and a husband with heart issues, and I was fearful of how long he would live.

In those times, Naren's silent support for me was extraordinary. By the end of 2002, we had significantly downsized the company, focusing only on maintaining our core products and the most reliable customers. We had cut costs everywhere possible. But the market was still not recovering, and we were running out of options.

Looking back, our renaming the company Quick Eagle Networks during the big downturn was like rearranging deck chairs on the *Titanic*. Major telecom customers could not find us on their internal list under that name, and our salespeople complained.

In the end, the whole idea of reverse IPO did not work out. But it was a choice we made. It was the bet we took.

In business school, they teach you about not throwing 'good money after bad,' but when it's your company—your creation—it's hard to let go. After the 1999 privatization battle, I did not give up. But by 2004, four years of leading Digital Link after the market collapse had left me feeling out of breath. I had seen everything—the good and the bad, the full cycle of a technology company. Maybe I was running out of steam. I would read motivational books to cheer me up so that I could walk into the office with purpose every day. There was no time for fakery.

In April 2004, Naren and I met with my CFO, Naresh Kapahi. Naren told him that he could not see me running the company any longer. Naresh offered to run the company for us. However, he wanted the freedom to make decisions; he did not want me second-guessing him from my corner office. At the time, Naren and I were the only stakeholders. I was left with a hard decision: I either stay or let go completely.

I quit from my CEO role that month. There was no farewell, no celebration of my twenty years of achievements. I hadn't predicted any of this. When I left, I felt I had given it my all. I didn't shed tears, nor did I feel sorry for myself. It was simply how the chips fell.

In his role as the new CEO, Naresh proved skilled at negotiations and controlling costs. He kept a few engineers and pared down operations even further, but the environment remained tough. Naresh viewed it as an opportunity, but then, despite his efforts, sales did not recover, and the company continued losing money.

By the end of 2005, the decision to shut down the company was made. Even though I had moved on, it marked the end of my twenty-year journey. We chose an orderly shutdown rather than declaring bankruptcy, even though it meant paying employees and creditors out of our own pockets. There was little discussion about it between Naren and me—we simply did what we felt was right. Naresh negotiated settlements with vendors, paying them a fraction of what was owed but ensuring they weren't left empty-handed. We also paid off the employees.

Finally, in 2006, we shut the doors. Naresh handled the shutdown process from start to finish—his final responsibility before closing this chapter. The fact that we'd paid all our bills was personally gratifying, though we never made that information public. Bankruptcy would have been easier, but it has a way of staying with you, tainting your reputation. At the time, we weren't thinking about our futures—we simply believed it was the right thing to do. Later, we both served on boards of companies. As a venture capitalist and board member of private and public companies, Naren could not have done so cleanly had he been associated with a bankruptcy. I, too, continued to serve on finance committees for nonprofit organizations, where integrity mattered.

By the time we shut down, I had witnessed the full cycle of Silicon Valley innovation, an experience that shaped me far more than I realized at the time. The end of my journey with Digital Link had made me totally fearless. It prepared me for my next adventure, something that would turn out to be even more competitive.

Someone recently asked, 'After Digital Link, why didn't you start another company?'

I surprised myself with my answer: 'I would have—had I not discovered bridge.'

PART V

A NEW CHAPTER: BRIDGE

IN DECEMBER 2014, I FOUND MYSELF SITTING ACROSS from Cezary Balicki in the finals of the North American Bridge Championship. Balicki was one of the top-ranked Polish players and among the thirty best in the world. His partner, Zmudzinski, was the second-ranked Polish player.

Bridge tournaments are like the Olympics—fierce, unpredictable, and requiring mental agility and mastery developed over decades. I wasn't looking to prove myself. At fifty-four, I simply wanted to take on something invigorating and challenging.

Balicki was an imposing figure: large, red-faced, with a broad forehead and bald pate. He was animated, intense, and deeply immersed in the game. The Polish pair used a bidding system called Polish Club, which I was unfamiliar with. It is used widely in Poland but less common internationally. In high-level tournaments, players sit on either side of a screen—a barrier that prevents any body language being exchanged between partners. Communication is strictly verbal or written, ensuring fairness.

A bidding system in bridge is a structured way for partners to communicate their hands and strategies. You can create your own rules in a bidding system as long as you disclose them to your opponents. Players are allowed to ask opponents any questions about their bids—no secretive communication. I was a relative novice, and my understanding of different bidding systems was far less developed than most players at that level.

As the match progressed, I started asking questions about the Polish Club system. Balicki answered in writing, as required, but with increasing irritation. He scribbled notes explaining the system, his frustration evident. On the final hand, he bid a grand slam—a contract requiring him to win all thirteen tricks. Grand slams are rare in bridge, and a big deal. But they were no dummies. Against a grand slam, my natural lead should have been a trump card, but instead I played a different suit.

Balicki stared at my lead card for a long time. He was either suspicious or confused—I still don't know which. But in that moment, his judgment faltered. He read my play and assumed I had no trump card. He didn't account for the fact that a newer player like myself wouldn't know what card I should have led against the grand slam. When he played his first trump, it played directly into my hand. His mistake cost them the grand slam, and my team won the match.

Looking back on that day, I recognize that Balicki gave me an invaluable lesson—not just in bridge, but in business and in life. In high-pressure situations, losing your cool puts you at a disadvantage. Your brain doesn't function well, your judgment becomes impaired, and you are unable to think strategically. Had Balicki remained patient, calmly explaining and maintaining his focus, he might have won the match—and possibly the tournament.

I understand why he was frustrated. Facing a novice who asked detailed questions in a national championship must have been irritating. He may have thought, *What is she doing here? Doesn't she belong in the amateur tournaments? Why should I waste my time with this person?* But his impatience led to a grave mistake, and that mistake cost him the game. The lesson is simple: Keep your wits about you and maintain a rational frame of mind. Once you lose that, you risk making many more mistakes.

Bad judgment and lack of patience often lead to bad decisions—and sometimes, unethical behavior. During the match, Balicki was unusually animated, and his partner made uncharacteristic plays, failing to follow percentage-based strategies. Even as I sat across from them, the bridge community suspected them of cheating. As a coda to this story, Balicki and Zmudzinski were later banned after being caught cheating in a major tournament.

Whenever I feel myself growing frustrated in a tournament or in life, I remind myself of that moment at the table. I picture Balicki, red-faced, scribbling notes to me as if instructing a toddler, and I remind myself to breathe, smile, and keep my cool.

In retrospect, this was one of the best memories of the more passionate phase of my life. Bridge became my primary focus in the years after Digital Link, offering a new challenge, a new arena for competition, and a new way to test my resilience.

The Beginning of Bridge

I FIRST SAW BRIDGE PLAYED WHEN I WAS A TEENAGER IN India. We would go to the homes of our uncles and aunts for our cousins' weddings, and in the late afternoons, I'd watch the men gather. They'd sit around drinking beer and eating hot pakoras with chutney, and they would play this card game with complete focus—no chitchat or laughter. I didn't understand what they were doing, but I was fascinated by their concentration and the mysterious language they used: 'one no-trump,' 'three spades,' 'double.' It seemed so sophisticated compared to the simple card games I knew. I would hover around, watching the cards being arranged and played, not understanding the rules but sensing there was something special about this game. Ladies never joined in. It was a men's game, I understood.

Bridge was popular in engineering colleges in India, but women had no exposure to it. It was only played in male dorms. The gender separation was very strict back then, and we never went inside their dorms, day or night. I imagined the men would gather in their common rooms late into the night, playing and arguing over hands. I heard about bridge but never had the opportunity to learn even the ABCs of the game.

After Naren and I married, I found out that he played bridge; he had learned it at IIT. I was intrigued. He had a close friend from Stanford whose wife was also interested in learning bridge, so we arranged to play together. Naren and his friend taught us ladies, patiently explaining bidding systems and play concepts. We listened some but learned mostly by playing and making mistakes. And it was all fun.

I still remember the excitement of understanding how a finesse worked or predicting who held what cards based on bidding patterns. Naren and I were always driven in whatever we did, and bridge was no exception. We weren't satisfied with just playing socially—we wanted to improve. We started going to the Palo Alto Bridge Club, where the atmosphere was far more serious than friendly living room games.

This required taking our bridge skills to another level, and it was intimidating. One evening early on, I picked up my hand with six cards in clubs and 'slipped,' opening with two clubs. Then, forgetting that I'd opened with two clubs, I indicated a strong hand, which I did not have. Naren was confused, and so were the other two players at our table. In the end, when the cards got played and they saw that I did not have a strong hand, they called the director. Oh, it made us even more nervous that a higher-level authority was summoned, and it was noticed by the other players in the club. Both Naren and I were intimidated, as if we had committed a sin. You should have seen the looks on our faces.

The people at the Palo Alto club had been playing for years. They had partnerships and rarely forgot their simple bidding systems. We were rookies. Mastering bridge basics can take five years or more. At first, I was nervous every time we went to the club, worried about making mistakes, slowing down the game, or misplaying a hand. But I did not know that learning bridge is never-ending. After you master the basics, you progress to learning how to tell your partner what you have through subsequent bids, which gets a lot muddier. You have to remember which card was played by whom, as all thirteen cards get played out.

Eventually, we had to stop playing to run our companies and raise our children. Life was too busy with board meetings, customer visits, employee issues, and raising two daughters. Bridge simply fell to the bottom of our priority list. It happens easily—you intend to keep up with hobbies, but work expands to fill all available time. However, after Naren's heart attack in 1997, I made it my priority to reduce his stress level. I suggested, 'Why don't we start going to the bridge club again?' Bridge is all-encompassing—you forget about everything else while playing.

We started going back to the club once a week. I was still working with Jack, the CEO of Digital Link, so I would leave the office at five thirty, pick up Naren, and we'd head to the club for the seven o'clock game. We also started attending lessons given by Walter, one of the club directors. Each week, we learned something new: newer conventions, transfer bids, slam bidding techniques. Whatever the topic, we would later try to apply it in our games.

The Reno Breakthrough

IN MARCH 1998, THERE WAS A TOURNAMENT IN RENO. IT was a national championship event, five steps above club games. We were eager and excited but had no idea what we were stepping into.

Naren and I, along with one of his Stanford friends and his business partner, decided to compete as a foursome. I was the weakest player among us. We flew to Reno on Thursday, planning to stay for three nights, though the tournament ran for ten days. We played in the lowest-level side events, two tournaments a day. To our surprise, we won trophies—first place in each event. I still have those trophies in my study.

On the last day of our intended stay, we decided to challenge ourselves with a higher-level tournament. The open event was enormous, with hundreds of tables set up in a hotel ballroom. We peeked inside and got cold feet. How in the world could we compete in there? But at the last moment, we decided to register.

We hadn't been back at the club very long—probably only six or eight months, playing once a week. Compared to most participants in the ballroom, we were complete novices. Many players had been competing for five to ten years, accumulating hundreds of master points. We only had a handful of fractional points from club games. I was nervous as I sat down at the table and looked over the crowd of competition. The first pair we got assigned to play against was serious looking, with convention cards full of complex agreements we'd never seen. But once the playing cards were dealt and the bidding began, my focus sharpened.

After playing for four hours, we were done. We felt we had not played too badly. We walked to the front, where the officials were sitting, to see the scores on a flipchart. We scanned the listing, starting from the middle going up. Finally, we found ourselves at the top! We were first! We just could not believe it. Had we really played so well, or were we just lucky? We did not know.

Next we went and asked the officials for our trophy.

'Those are only for new player events,' they explained to us. 'Here you get master points!' In regular club games, placing first or second earns a fraction of a master point. But in Reno for this event, we each won twenty master points. We had hit a jackpot! We couldn't even keep our feet on the ground. We were so overjoyed.

We decided to rent a car and drive back that evening instead of flying out the next morning. The five-hour drive home was in utter silence. The four of us sat in awe, replaying the hands in our heads. We were hooked.

The Bridge Masters

Eddie Kantar, Bridge Magician

AFTER WE REPRIVATIZED DIGITAL LINK, I EXPLORED NEW ideas within the company. Silicon Valley executives loved their golf-tournament fundraising, for example, where they would spend a day at Pebble Beach or the Olympic Club, networking with other executives and raising money for charities. But I didn't play golf, and I never got into it. So, I decided to organize a bridge tournament fundraiser instead—something different, memorable, and appealing to a different crowd than the usual golf events.

For this, I needed to create a draw, someone important in the bridge world to give our event credibility. I found a renowned bridge expert's phone number through bridge connections and nervously cold-called him. Eddie Kantar (not the early twentieth-century entertainer) was one of the most accomplished bridge players in the world and a renowned bridge author. He won multiple world championships and wrote dozens of books on bridge technique. Meeting someone of his caliber opened my eyes to how deep the world of bridge went beyond our local club games.

My VP of marketing, a young but capable strategist, advised me to spend the first five minutes on the phone praising Eddie. 'Who doesn't like flattery?' he said. When I called, I was prepared with compliments about Eddie's books and championship record. But he immediately put me at ease with his warmth. He had the sweetest voice, reminiscent of Tom Perkins, who was always respectful despite his stature in venture capital. The first thing Eddie asked was where my accent was from. When I told him I was originally from India, he showed genuine interest, asking about the bridge scene back home.

I explained my idea for a charity bridge event to benefit a local school in East Palo Alto, a disadvantaged area just minutes from the wealthy Silicon Valley community. Eddie was enthusiastic about the idea. He also wanted his books distributed to every participant, with all proceeds going to the school. He said he didn't need any money beyond what I agreed to pay him. His generosity was remarkable. Eddie lived in Los Angeles, so I offered him accommodation options—either a hotel or staying at my house. He immediately chose the more personal option, asking why he would want to stay in a hotel. He and his wife stayed with us for several days.

We took them to Monterey in a limousine, thinking it appropriate for someone of his stature. In those days, we had just begun to enjoy the perks that came with Digital Link's success—things we weren't used to before. Both Naren and I were raised to be frugal, and we would still try to save a dollar whenever possible despite our financial success.

During Eddie's visit, we tried to introduce bridge to our daughters, but they weren't interested. They had watched Naren and me argue so much over bridge that they wanted no part of it. Anneka and Serena would roll their eyes whenever we started discussing bridge hands at the dinner table. 'Not bridge again,' they'd groan. They remember yelling matches that turned them off from the game entirely.

That's one thing about bridge partnerships—there are hardly any who don't argue. Not even 1 per cent of partnerships are argument-free. Bridge is too complex, with too many judgment calls and interpretations, for partners to always agree. Even world champions debate decisions after the game. Maybe that's why my daughters want nothing to do with it—they had already seen their parents debate everything else in life!

Eddie became a source of inspiration during his stay with us. He gave us a glimpse of what was possible in bridge. When we drove to Monterey, we played bridge in the limousine, and he was able to tell me what cards I had in my hand. We thought he was a magician. We couldn't even think at the level he was operating at. He was able to deduce what was in my hand based on the bidding and play. Once he saw his partner's hand (the dummy), he could figure out what cards the opponents held. It appeared he could reconstruct the entire hand with amazing accuracy. We didn't think in those ways at that stage of our development. Bridge has so many layers—inference, deduction, and psychology. That's what makes it so challenging and fascinating.

Eddie's level of card-reading skill comes after at least fifteen years of high-level bridge experience. If you play enough hands, see thousands of deals, then patterns emerge. You start to recognize distributions and card combinations. People say bridge is a game of experience, but not everyone becomes a Roger Federer or Tiger Woods of their field. Some players have that special knack for understanding the game in a way others can't match. Eddie passed away in 2022, but I'm grateful I had the opportunity to learn from him.

Someone recently asked me who my favorite bridge player is. I said, 'Zia.' Zia Mahmood is a Pakistani-born player now representing the United States, famous for his flamboyant style and table presence. I explained that he's such a good card reader. He has table sense. He takes calculated chances that others don't. He has a unique fluidity and has digested the game in a different way. Bridge isn't just about calculating odds, though that's part of it. The number of odds you need to know can be counted on two hands—that covers 90 per cent of situations. But sometimes the cards aren't distributed according to the odds, and that's when truly great players shine. They sense when to deviate from the percentages based on subtle clues from the bidding and play.

Expert Billy Miller

AFTER DIGITAL LINK SHUT DOWN IN 2006, I HAD MORE time for bridge. I started going to the club alone, playing with good bridge players who agreed to be my partners. They charged me to play with them, though much less than higher-level professionals charge now. One older gentleman at the club, Hamish Bennett, told me he didn't want to charge me anything beyond the table fee. He was wise and well respected at the club. He said he would introduce me to Billy Miller, suggesting I'd do well playing with him.

I didn't know anything about Billy Miller at the time. Hamish must have told Billy about me because when I showed up at a tournament in Santa Clara, Billy came over after the game, introduced himself, and offered to coach me. Before I agreed, I asked around about him. One lady, a bridge friend, told me, 'Be careful. Billy has made clients cry.' That was certainly an interesting introduction! Imagine paying someone who makes you cry! It's not exactly a typical sales pitch for a coach.

But I wasn't easily intimidated, and I decided to try working with him anyway. I knew the pros and cons, and I needed someone to coach me. He immediately started pulling me into his orbit. I began with the assumption that he could be tough—I liked that part. But I wasn't going to let anyone put me down; I knew how to push back. I couldn't allow myself to feel bad while playing.

I started playing in national tournaments with Billy as my coach and partner. He introduced me to major events held three times a year across America—spring, summer, and fall nationals, each in a different city. With him, I won three national championships. Billy was very goal-driven. He wanted us to win something tangible. He would tell me we needed to hire the best people for our team, which meant paying more money. As he put it, 'When people see the Gupta team, they should feel intimidated, not think we can be easily beaten.'

Billy was highly resourceful and showed remarkable agility. In 2017, at the nationals in Orlando, Florida, our star-studded team—including Zia—was eliminated on the very first day of the main event. This isn't uncommon in high-level bridge, but Billy immediately pivoted. Within hours, he recruited two young women on the spot so that our team could compete in the Mixed Team event, where every man must play with a woman partner. Naturally, I played with Billy.

The event lasted three or four days, and to our surprise, we won. It was another feather in my cap—a national championship victory. Watching Billy in action was incredible. He negotiated deals, hired new players within hours, and seamlessly restructured our team—all with my approval. One of the young women was barely twenty-four, and this was her first national win. Seeing her excitement reminded me of the thrill of my own early victories.

As I entered and trained for tournaments, bridge became expensive. To win a national championship, I not only hired top professionals but also participated in six regional tournaments to sharpen myself. I was now spending nearly $1 million a year and was away from home ninety days annually. By then, the kids had moved out, but Naren was still working and home by himself. The time commitment alone started taking a personal toll on our marriage. Eventually, I decided to put bridge on hold.

Billy was my coach and partner for ten years. He was a great bridge player, but he gave me less room for growth. Even though we won tournaments, I didn't feel I was progressing as fast. (I am an impatient sort.) When family circumstances allowed me to return to bridge, I began rethinking my bridge strategy. I realized I needed a coach who could help me understand the deeper layers of the game, not just react to situations. And that's when I reconnected with Morten.

Morten's Logic Supreme

BILLY FIRST INTRODUCED ME TO MORTEN WHEN HE HIRED him and his famous son for a tournament. Morten's son Dennis is now considered one of the top five bridge players in the world. He learned bridge from his dad, and they played together until Dennis became a ranked player in professional circuits. Morten, however, spends most of his time in Denmark, teaching schoolchildren how to play bridge, for free. He is modest, patient, and deeply passionate about teaching.

A few years ago, I crossed paths with Morten again at a tournament in San Francisco. I was restarting my approach to bridge, though I wasn't entirely sure how or why—perhaps I was rediscovering myself. Winning more tournaments wouldn't add much to my résumé, but learning would. I had already won national tournaments, and was placed in the top five in an international event. Winning was nice, but it felt empty without intellectual growth.

Morten had traveled to San Francisco with a friend who had end-stage cancer, and they needed to stay in a home rather than a hotel room. I offered my Silicon Valley home, assuring Morten that Veronica, my assistant for sixteen years, would be there to help with anything they needed. Morten and his friend stayed at my house, and Veronica drove them around, showing them Stanford and Apple's campus.

After the tournament, once Morten and his friend had left, I told Veronica that I wasn't sure what to do about my bridge. She suggested I talk to Morten about being my coach, noting that he was not only a great teacher but also a good person. I asked Morten, and he agreed. Since then, I've had Morten and some of his finest young Danish students in tournaments with me. It has become a tenacious team of younger players, and I have raised the bar for myself as a bridge player.

Learning bridge from Morten has turned out to be a truly enriching experience. He approaches bridge as a puzzle—an endless thought exercise. He emphasizes logic above all else. 'Always understand the logic,' he says. 'Bidding conventions have nuances. You can bid this way or that way. If neither approach works well in a given hand, just bid what makes sense to you.'

Here's an example. Our bidding system says that if I open with one diamond bid, and my partner responds with two clubs, this is a two-over-one convention, meaning we are committed to reaching a game contract. Conventionally, if I have five diamonds, I am obligated to rebid two diamonds. But Morten taught me that I don't have to follow this rule blindly. Instead, I should think about what information my partner needs most. If my diamonds are weak but I have better spades, I can bid two spades to show at least four spades, even though I have five diamonds. Quality matters more than quantity.

These are the nuances of bidding. You don't follow rules just because they exist—you think critically about what makes the most sense in the moment. It is the freedom to sensibly bend the rules that makes bridge exciting.

Once I started thinking about bridge through Morten's approach, the game became simpler, more interesting, and more intuitive. I started enjoying it more. He had rekindled my passion. Today, bridge consumes me in a good way. When I'm preparing for a tournament, I shut out the world. There isn't room in my mind for much else. I can ask Morten a question, and he always answers like a teacher—with kindness and respect.

Billy's approach was good when I was a relative beginner who dared to enter top bridge competitions. Through him, I learned by mimicking. That is how children start learning. Bridge is a very complex endeavor to teach by just playing tournaments. It's like appearing in exams without taking classes. With Billy, I won tournaments when I knew so little.

But I had advanced now. Morten came into my life at the right time. He provides explanations, which make learning and remembering easier. When I make a mistake, he says, 'I just want to know what was going through your mind.' If I can still remember my reasoning, I explain it to him. He listens, then says, 'Now I understand. It helps me see why you did what you did.'

Morten also changed my approach to teamwork. With Billy, he managed the other team members, and I chose not to be involved. With Morten, it's different. He insists we work transparently and cohesively as a team. I never thought much about the other team members when I was with Billy. Now, I regularly interact with all of them. Rather than staying in separate hotel rooms, we rent an Airbnb to stay together. We make breakfast for each other, discuss strategies, and admit mistakes we made to learn from them—that's team playing. I wish I had adopted these skills while running Digital Link.

Less than three months after Naren's passing in December 2021, my team won silver in the prestigious Vanderbilt—the most prized national bridge event. The tournament took place in Reno, twenty-four years after Naren's and my first amateur win there.

Ten Bridge Lessons
A Metaphor For Life

WHEN I STEPPED AWAY FROM DIGITAL LINK, I DIDN'T STOP competing—I simply changed arenas. Bridge deepened my thinking, stretched my intuition, and reconnected me with the discipline of play. Competing against the best in bridge is like an IPO roadshow—high stakes, intense scrutiny, and no room for error. The timeline for mistakes is much shorter—just seven minutes per hand. This accelerates the learning too.

At the next level, bridge became a lens through which I began to view life itself. From this game, I've learned valuable lessons that apply well beyond the card table. The principles of good bridge map cleanly to business, relationships, and most aspects of life. Here are some of the rules I have taken away from my time with bridge. Maybe they can help you too.

Lesson One: *Let Go of the Past.* How often do we waste energy thinking about past decisions we can't change? Once you make a decision, don't regret it—not even for a second. The hand is over. Legendary bridge player Bob Hamman once said, 'Don't fight yesterday's war.' Always look forward because you can't change what happened. Looking back adds no value. This ability to let go of the past and focus on the present is an invaluable skill.

Lesson Two: *Don't Overthink.* Your brain can get thinking about the what and why when you need to be applying yourself. People told me for years, 'You're overthinking,' but I never quite understood it. Deeper knowledge comes very gradually. You know what you know, and beyond that you need to trust your instincts. It's like hitting back the tennis ball during a match.

You can't start thinking how to hit the ball when the ball is coming at you. In that moment, you need to trust your past learnings and the instincts you've developed. If you find that you're overthinking, pausing and taking a deep breath helps. Calm and relaxed minds make better, quicker decisions.

Lesson Three: *Selective Learning.* You can't absorb every lesson from every mistake. During a week-long tournament, my brain can retain no more than a handful of key lessons. Our minds can't hold on to every subtle detail from every hand. If you remember even two lessons from each tournament and apply them to future games, you'll be a winner. Knowledge accumulates and compounds only if you can retain it.

Lesson Four: *Make Decisions with Imperfect Information.* I first learned this lesson with my startup. When running Digital Link, I often had to make difficult decisions with limited information. Should we enter a new market? Should we develop this product or not? Should we hire this executive? We would gather the available information, weigh probabilities, commit to a course of action, and course correct if the situation demanded it. Likewise, in bridge there are limited bidding rules to determine who might hold what cards, especially as the hand progresses. But there are hundreds of millions of ways cards can be dealt. You have to make decisions based on the information available and move forward.

Lesson Five: *Focus Matters.* With bridge, you must be able to zoom in when needed. There's an Indian saying about a guru who asked his archery student, 'Do you see that bird?' The student replied, 'No.' The guru asked, 'What do you see?' And the student said, 'I see the eye of the bird.' He was so focused that nothing else existed for him in that moment. In bridge, you focus only on what matters right now. Competitive bridge tests your ability to live in the present to an extreme. That is mindfulness.

Lesson Six: *Read the Cards.* This is when zooming out is needed. Eddie Kantar and other masters in bridge are good at reading the cards. It's about keeping peripheral vision alive to learn what's happening at the table—who has what based on what cards have been played and how. Also what a player could be thinking about when they take too long, or what others might still be confused about. Yes, you should understand the logic and conventions. But you must also trust your instincts, allowing your brain space to think and read the cards.

Lesson Seven: *Break the Rules.* Morten's lesson about not always playing by the rules is also essential for running a business. There is always a textbook move—one that you might read about in a business school case study. But many times, if you break convention, you change the game—and then you win, like I did with Balicki. In that case, it was inadvertent. I played a hand incorrectly and broke the rule. This changed his thinking and broke his cool. He made a mistake, and my team won.

Lesson Eight: *Value Partnership.* One of the most important lessons bridge taught me about business is the value of teamwork and partnership. In bridge, you must trust your partner completely to be effective. The same applies in business. At Digital Link, I learned to trust my executive team, just as I rely on my bridge partner. When you click with your executives, it does wonders for the business. No CEO succeeds alone, just as no bridge player wins tournaments alone. And those partnerships need to be cultivated and nurtured.

Lesson Nine: *Stay Grounded.* Bridge also taught me humility. No matter how good you become, you'll make mistakes. The best players in the world make errors. The key is learning from them without dwelling on mistakes—something that served me well as a CEO. When we made missteps at Digital Link, I didn't waste time blaming others. As the CEO, the buck stopped with me.

Lesson Ten: *Keep Your Cool.* Perhaps most importantly, bridge taught me to keep my cool under pressure. Business, and life in general, often puts you in high-pressure situations where losing your composure can be disastrous. Whether negotiating with investors, handling a crisis, or facing competitors, maintaining a clear head pays off. I've applied these bridge lessons to my interactions with others. The game continues to shape how I think, make decisions, and relate to others. It's more than a hobby—it's a framework for understanding complex systems and human behavior.

Looking back on my journey—from that curious girl watching men play bridge in India to competing at national championships—I realize that bridge has given me far more than the thrill of competition. It has given me tools for success and rich associations with different sets of people whom I have grown close to over the years. In bridge, learning never stops. It compounds over time. For anyone looking to improve their strategic thinking and decision-making abilities, I can't recommend bridge highly enough. It's more than a game. It's a lifelong teacher, a meditation in awareness, decision-making, and grace when it matters most.

PART VI

TWO TIGERS' LOVE STORY

ON 25 DECEMBER 2021, MY HUSBAND NAREN PASSED AWAY. We had been married for forty-seven years. He died suddenly of a heart attack while resting peacefully at my sister's house in Indian Land, South Carolina.

Naren had wanted to come with me to visit my sister on our way home after vacationing in Florida. She had just lost her husband, and he felt obligated to be there for her. On Christmas morning, we went out looking for a breakfast place, not wanting to trouble my sister. Nothing was open, so we ate at home. After breakfast, Naren went for a shower. Then it was my turn. When I came out, he was lying on the bed. Something was wrong. I touched his chest, but he was gone.

I was in shock. My sister called the paramedics—I didn't think of that as the first thing. When they came, I couldn't recall the word for a defibrillator, a device that might have saved his life. So I didn't know if they did not have a defibrillator or didn't use it. I was distraught. When they could not revive him, they decided to take him in their van to the nearest hospital in North Carolina.

First I made a call to my children, who were still vacationing in Florida. Then I went to the hospital. An hour later, the ER doctor came and said, 'I'm sorry. We could not revive him. We are sorry for your loss.'

Naren was moved into another room. I spent time with his body, alone, as Dr. Croke advised. Surprisingly, no tears rolled down. Looking at his motionless face, I said things to him that made no sense. After the kids arrived, we started thinking of the next step, how to take his body home.

Once I was home, I prioritized meeting with Naren's Nexus team members, who were already gathered for their annual meeting in early January. I needed to learn what was happening there, and what my involvement would or would not be. I had a huge financial stake in Nexus, and still do. Afterward, I had to arrange Naren's celebration of life.

Seems too businesslike, doesn't it? But that's who I am. Now, almost four years since, I live with the memories of our caring yet contentious lives together. When faced with tough problems, I still ask, 'What would have Naren said?'

Two Tigers

AT HIS CELEBRATION OF LIFE, I CALLED OUR RELATIONSHIP a two-tiger marriage. A perfect example of this was three years after we got married, when we bought our beautiful home in an upscale neighborhood in Silicon Valley—Sharon Heights. During a trip to India, we purchased a large framed Indian textile to decorate a wall in the new home.

We both agreed to hang it on the long dining room wall. But we could not agree on how high from the floor it should be hung. We called each other names over our aesthetic sense, but neither of us budged. The painting simply sat on the floor, leaning against the wall, till we moved out.

There were many more instances when we stuck to our guns—like how we wanted to raise our kids. He wanted to be more strict with them, while I had a more relaxed approach.

There's a reason why, in the wild, there is only one alpha in a pride. Stability depends on the peace imposed by a single leader, a strong force. A two-tiger marriage requires constant give and take—neither partner is ever the alpha forever. And that, I believe, was the strength of our relationship. Each partner is aware of the pushback, the resistance, the negotiation. It forces growth, adaptation, and ultimately, a better life together.

Ours was a marriage that, in many ways, evolved, and in some ways did not. We often butted heads, both of us stubborn, but we worked through our differences over forty-seven years. I wouldn't say we mellowed much over time. The only haunting ghost was Naren's health, but he had outlived the initial five-year prognosis by fifteen years. As they say in Las Vegas lingo, we were playing with house money.

And that picture on the floor? The one that sat for three years because neither of us would compromise? Ten years later, when we moved to our house in Woodside—an even bigger home with more walls, more space for family, and more room for our two big personalities—Naren said, 'Decoration is now your department.' As I set up our new home, he may have made a few comments, but I was the tiger in charge of decorating. I smile remembering this.

Arranged Marriage

OUR PARENTS INTRODUCED US THROUGH THE traditional process, but neither of them could pressure us into marriage. We were both strongheaded, and our individual parents knew it. For both of us, arranged marriage was the expectation—as it was for 90 per cent of the people we knew in India. One of my cousins opted for a love marriage, and it was not considered a good choice by the family.

Naren and I had an arranged marriage, but it was far from the rigid, predetermined arrangement that many assume. When you tell people in the United States that yours was an arranged marriage, they assume your parents made the decision and you had no choice. That was not the case with us. We were arranged, but we also chose each other.

There was also the matter of a dowry. My parents didn't save up for a dowry, and matches they would find in India would require them to provide substantial money. American prospects generally didn't ask for a dowry, which was part of their appeal. My parents also genuinely thought I would be happier in America and that the country would suit my personality. In America, I would be able to pursue education and a profession without being too tied to family and the conservative culture of India. In a way, my parents traded the dowry money for my education. I guess this was a vote of confidence in me that also intensified my desire to succeed.

Partnership, Partnership, and Partnership

NAREN AND I BECAME IMMERSED IN THE SILICON VALLEY of the 1970s and '80s as the region transformed from a sleepy agricultural hub into the technology epicenter of the world. As engineers, we loved living in a place that was on the cutting edge of our field, surrounded by brilliant minds from around the globe. When I worked at BNR, we socialized with sharp, unconventional thinkers—hackers who talked about financial schemes, technology, and everything in between. Naren picked up on that before me and started his company. Slowly, we acquired the knack for cocktail party talk, learning just enough about sports to pass as natural Americans.

Naren and I became not just bridge partners but partners in crime. We were deeply committed to our professional growth and occasionally sought each other's advice even if we didn't always like what the other person said. Our mutual push—'You could do better'—created unnecessary tension in our relationship, but it also propelled us forward. Together, our outcomes were greater than the sum of our individual parts. That pattern continued through nearly five decades of life together.

Our marriage for the first ten years, when we were still adjusting to each other, entailed many activities, including vacation travel. We discovered we were two adventurous souls. And over the next forty-seven years, we explored more than a hundred countries together. I remember our first time in Paris—we nearly slept in our rental car because we hadn't made a reservation at any bed-and-breakfast. And yes, we often returned from trips not speaking to each other. Travel tests a relationship in unexpected ways.

Six months after I started Digital Link, Naren dragged me for a trip to Machu Picchu for a one-week hike on the Inca Trail. It felt like leaving a six-month-old baby home alone. The trail was all-consuming, and we hadn't trained at all. But we were young and could handle it. Stepping away from the grind of business worries rejuvenated me.

On the long flight back from Machu Picchu, we played bridge to pass time. We had traveled with another couple, our friends, who also played bridge. At one point, when Naren criticized my play, I got so mad that I threw my cards at him, and the cards went flying through the aisles of the aircraft. We laughed about it later.

Our love for travel became a family ritual, especially after the kids arrived. It was how I got quality time with them. We traveled so much that we never saved—not until Naren's company went public.

We also took up skiing together and enjoyed its thrill. The first time I went skiing, I could not even come down the bunny slope. I had to be brought down in a toboggan by a ski patrol. I was shivering with cold because of slipping and falling in the snow over and over. Naren had skied only a couple of times before. He insisted it would be better next time. When I went the second time, I was fearful, remembering my first experience. I snowplowed with all my might and inched forward. To my surprise, I did not fall. My confidence grew, so we went again, and then again. We also taught our kids to ski at a very young age. I remember going down the half-pipe with the girls following me, experiencing the cold, refreshing breeze. For people like us, who hadn't seen snow until our mid-twenties, the whole rigamarole of putting heavy ski boots on, bundling up, and learning to ski was tough. But we toughened up, together.

We were both adventure seekers, lovers of bridge and travel. What a partnership we had—tackling the ups and downs of three different businesses. We were intellectual equals amid our conflicts.

Tiger Cubs

NAREN AND I WANTED CHILDREN, BUT ONCE WE STARTED trying, I suffered two miscarriages. We figured we were not fated to have kids.

Then, when my focus shifted to raising money for my new company, I became pregnant with Anneka. The timing was far from perfect, but we were overjoyed. We had been married for thirteen years at that point. But I had to continue pushing the company forward, as I had accepted venture funding.

Naren never asked me to stop working—except once. After Anneka, we tried for a second child, but I was not getting pregnant. Naren asked me if, to reduce stress, I would consider not working. This was very hard for him to say, I could tell. Ultimately, I decided to keep on working.

When Serena arrived five years later, our plate became even more full. She was another welcome bundle of joy. We both had incredibly busy lives with high-octane careers, but we managed to balance family with our ambitions. As I mentioned, Naren had his ideas about how to raise our kids, and I had mine. We never completely agreed.

But they both turned out to be tigers too.

A Life Well Lived

RIGHT UP UNTIL THE END OF HIS LIFE IN DECEMBER 2021, Naren was at the top of his game. His venture fund, Nexus Venture Partners, was finally thriving after fifteen years, growing in reputation and influence. He'd dreamed of creating an Indian unicorn—a company valued at over a billion dollars—and he could see several emerging from his portfolio. In fact, one of his companies, PubMatic, achieved that vaunted figure in public market valuation early in 2021, just months before he passed.

The last four months of his life were particularly joyful. After COVID, we were finally able to travel again. The day before he passed, we had just returned from a week-long family vacation in Florida. He loved it so much that he declared that we should make it an annual ritual.

He canoed for two hours with Anneka as the main paddler. He loved being with our daughters. In the evenings, he was serving margaritas two glasses at a time, as fast as I could churn them out. We embraced the tropical lifestyle, leaving behind the stresses and worries of our everyday lives. This was how he wanted life to be.

Two days before he passed, he played online bridge with his favorite people: his brother Ash and the famous Zia, the Tiger Woods of bridge, whom our daughters teasingly called 'Dad's boyfriend.' Sitting on a beach chair outside our Airbnb, overlooking the water, playing bridge with his closest friends—life couldn't get any better.

The day before he passed, the two of us went canoeing alone in the Gulf of Mexico. The water was shallow around the delta, so we had to be careful not to get our canoe stuck. Naren clicked picture after picture: white egrets, blue herons, cormorants, and pelicans, either floating in the water or soaring above us in formation. The delta was half submerged, with green leaves on thin red stems—mangroves in the making. Amateur fishermen with rickety equipment cast their lines from their boats, though the fish weren't biting that day. Then, we flew to my sister's place in South Carolina, where he spent the last moments of his life.

These are the memories of Naren that I live with.

PART VII

THE DAUGHTERS

MY LIFE HAS BEEN FULL OF CHALLENGES AND FASCINATING adventures. One of the greatest of these was when, to our surprise, I became pregnant with Anneka. The timing wasn't ideal—I had just launched Digital Link. Serena came as another surprise. She turned two just as Digital Link was preparing for its IPO. We hadn't expected to have a second child—I was forty-two and thought I was the oldest mother ever.

Throughout their childhood, my daughters knew that Mommy also ran a business. I was constantly balancing family life and demanding work. Since I had my kids late, I perhaps enjoyed them and valued their presence more than a young mother would. I had the advantage of patience—and perspective. At work, I was the CEO, and at home, a mother. It was enjoyable but emotionally overwhelming, especially when I traveled.

The girls often visited my workplace when they were young. One afternoon when Serena was six or seven, her nanny brought her to my office after school. Thinking she would enjoy the visual parts of running a company, I showed her the finished products in metal casings, brochures, the manufacturing floor, components, and how we packaged and shipped them.

After about an hour, she surprised me by asking, 'Mommy, what do people do with the box?' She wasn't interested in the process—she wanted to understand the purpose. It was an excellent question that made me realize how differently she thought.

Serena remained inquisitive as she grew up, always asking tough questions. She was also highly competitive, striving to excel—perhaps because she placed her older sister, Anneka, on a pedestal and wanted to keep up. Despite their five-year age gap, their sibling dynamic was shaped by mutual admiration.

We traveled extensively as a family. Some of our best trips were on National Geographic ships led by scientists and explorers, giving us an insider's view of some of the most remote and exotic environments on Earth. We visited the Galápagos Islands to see what Charles Darwin had written about in *On the Origin of Species*, standing just a foot away from blue-footed boobies.

But our favorite trip was to Antarctica. We flew to southern Chile, crossed the torturous Drake Passage by boat, and reached the icy continent. The National Geographic crew organized a polar plunge into freezing waters, calling it the 'Antarctic Plunge.' Naren, who rarely showed restraint to protect his weak heart, opted out. Anneka, Serena, and I lined up for the jump. The shock of the cold stunned all of my senses. It was crazy—especially with me being over fifty.

Earlier, I wrote about our nannies. Ginger stands out—she raised the girls until they were ready for college, staying with us for twelve years. Most evenings, after I returned from work totally exhausted, Ginger gave me instructions. There would be a list of tasks: Make sure the girls brush their teeth, check their homework, and be sure they go to bed by nine. That irritated me.

One evening, I blurted out in front of the kids, 'Ginger doesn't understand how tired I get. She goes back to her cottage and puts her feet up.'

When I came home the next day, Ginger asked to speak with me privately. Apparently, Serena had carried my message to her. Ginger asked, 'What do you mean that I put my feet up?' Taken out of context, I understood why Ginger would be offended. Ginger was on duty twelve hours a day; her list was to ensure that the kids did not get up tired the next morning. I apologized.

There was another incident Ginger shared when Serena was around four or five—not yet in school full-time. One afternoon, Serena had a friend over, and the two were sitting down to eat lunch that Ginger had prepared. Serena was either taking her time or not eating at all. When Ginger commanded, 'Serena, please finish your lunch,' she responded, 'I don't have to eat lunch because you're telling me to. You're just a servant.'

Ginger had tears in her eyes when she recounted the story to me the next day. I was, of course, shocked. Quickly, I said, 'Do you think I taught her that? I'm not sure where she picked up the word "servant".' Then I pointed out, 'Serena doesn't watch television with us.' Ginger was the one who allowed them to watch TV, where Serena likely would have heard the term. Ginger quickly realized the connection.

Anneka was calmer, and Ginger taught her how to crochet, which Anneka still does to relax, just like Ginger. Serena was more like me—a bit of a troublemaker. One apple did not fall far from the tree.

It's worth mentioning another incident from when Serena was still quite young. I took her to a grocery store, rushing around to pick up ingredients for dinner. On the way back to the car, Serena had a quiet look on her face. She climbed in, and I fastened her seatbelt. When we arrived home, I opened the car door for her to jump out—and candies spilled out from her folded dress. She had helped herself to treats.

Immediately, I flashed back to my own childhood and the candyman at my first school. I knew that temptations are hard to resist.

Rather than scolding her, I said, 'Serena, tomorrow we'll go and return the candies.'

I feel that girls are harshly punished for mischief compared to boys, and I did not want her spirit crushed. Besides, boldness and aggression are needed to break limits and achieve what others think are impossible.

As our daughters grew, I realized they were getting too heavy a dose of Western culture through their Catholic school education and not enough of Indian culture. For elementary school, they both attended Sacred Heart in Menlo Park—a decision that felt natural to us, as private Catholic schools were common in India. But soon I felt they needed a counterbalance.

From the beginning, our daughters revealed distinct personalities. Anneka was levelheaded, direct in her approach, thoughtful, and measured, while Serena was jittery and impulsive, but also creative and inquisitive, always asking the hard questions. Neither shied away from new experiences or stepping out of their comfort zones—a motto that Naren and I lived by: Don't get too comfortable.

When they brought home pictures of Jesus Christ and Mary, it reminded me of my own boarding school days. Wanting them to have some 'Indian dosage' in their lives, I looked for ways to introduce them to our heritage. Since we didn't practice religion beyond Diwali celebrations and rarely spoke Hindi to them, Indian classical dance seemed like the perfect way to connect them to their roots.

Every Sunday, we took them to an Indian dance teacher—actually a doctor who taught dance purely for the love of it. The girls initially enjoyed it, and I loved seeing them perform in traditional outfits to Indian music. We watched Bollywood films at home as another way to stay connected to Indian culture, and when we visited India, I would buy them special clothes for their dance performances.

This went on for years—until Serena, who hated discipline, rebelled. 'We don't have to learn dancing from Maya,' she declared one day. 'I can choreograph and teach Anneka.' She began choreographing dances to Hindi songs despite not understanding the lyrics. Sometimes, she would ask me, 'What do these words mean?' What surprised me most was Anneka's willingness to learn from her younger sister. Despite being five years older, she never had an ego about it. She happily followed Serena's direction and choreography. I admired this in Anneka just as much as I admired Serena's creativity and insistence on making Indian dance her own. This arrangement lasted into their late teens, and soon they became known for their dancing within our extended family.

As I would later observe, Anneka's willingness to follow reflected her innate ability to lead and collaborate. Most older siblings wouldn't learn from their younger ones, but Anneka had no problem with it. She could follow just as easily as she could lead—a sign of someone comfortable with herself and her abilities.

Though different in temperament, both girls had strong personalities and were never afraid to stand their ground. They also proved resistant to the typical 'tiger mom' aspirations. When Anneka was young, I suggested she take Kumon classes to strengthen her math skills. She firmly refused, saying, 'Mom, I will never take Kumon.' She hated rote learning and repetition.

Later, when I saw how math was taught in her high school and college, I understood her reasoning. Anneka was trained to solve problems and think creatively—very different from my own education, which emphasized memorization. With Serena, we didn't even dare to suggest Kumon, knowing her response would likely be even stronger.

For high school, both girls attended Menlo School. There, Anneka developed a deep respect for her karate instructor, Mr. Chandler. When he later became her college counselor, she refused our suggestion to hire a private counselor, saying, 'No way. That would be disrespectful to my favorite teacher.'

As she entered high school, Anneka's senior prom became an introduction to American culture for both Naren and me. Anneka and four or five of her girlfriends attended the dance—without male dates. When other mothers gossiped about it, I realized this was not the norm in America. In India, girls dancing with girls would be usual. But Anneka had no problem standing out, and she and her friends didn't need boys to have a great time. As the firstborn, she constantly taught us the real American way of how teens were raised.

Despite not being particularly athletic, Anneka sought out physical challenges. One summer, she attended a climbing camp in the Rocky Mountains. When she returned, she casually mentioned how her ponytail had gotten entangled in the rappelling rope, and an instructor had to free her. She told the story nonchalantly, but I suspected there was more to it. Regardless, she made it out in one piece.

Academically, Anneka excelled seemingly without effort. Serena, in contrast, struggled more but persevered—much like I had at Roorkee. Serena was deeply disappointed when she didn't get into Stanford and had to 'settle' for UC Berkeley. (Of course, she did well in high school, even if she lived in her sister's intellectual shadow.) We all knew Cal was one of the best public universities in the world. Anneka wisely observed, 'Berkeley is much better for Serena. At Stanford, every kid feels inadequate.'

In the end, Berkeley campus upheld Serena's slightly chaotic energy and nurtured her adventurous spirit far more than Stanford's palm-lined quads would have.

Navigating College and Career

AS ANNEKA PROGRESSED THROUGH COLLEGE, SHE thought deeply about her path and future. She initially opted for majoring in physics but found it too difficult after her first year. She approached me after freshman summer, mentioning that some friends were studying international communications. Then she quickly added, 'I know you and Dad will never let me do that.'

I asked her to show me Stanford's description of the major. After reading the requirements, I pointed out, 'You're going from a very high-level subject to a much lower one. Will you be challenged enough?'

She eventually found a compromise: mathematics and computational sciences. It was rigorous but not as extreme as physics. We looked at Stanford's career data, which showed graduates from this program landing roles at top companies like Apple, Meta, Microsoft, and Google. Anneka decided it made sense for her.

While Anneka followed a steady path, Serena leaned toward a riskier one. She thrived in the startup world, often gravitating toward fast-moving companies. One summer at Berkeley, she announced she wouldn't be coming home—she had joined a project with another student and a professor to develop an online homework collaboration platform. Naren, always cautious, asked about this student leading the project. Serena explained, 'He has already graduated. He's starting this company.'

Over the following weeks, discussions continued. Naren, thinking like a venture capitalist, asked, 'If the company becomes successful, how much equity will you receive?' Serena admitted they had never discussed it. Like many young people, she was excited to work at a startup, without worrying about ownership. Naren pointed out that unpaid work should come with some equity. Serena, keenly aware of fairness, realized the situation might be unjust. After she pressed the team leader, he eventually proposed she receive 10 per cent while he would retain 90 per cent of equity. The professor would receive nothing. Concerned, Serena discussed this with the professor—who was furious.

Serena called Naren. 'Dad, my professor would like to talk to you. Can you come to Cal?'

We met in the cafeteria, where Naren explained equity to the professor. Days later, Serena told us all parties had gone their separate ways—the deal was unacceptable. It was an early entrepreneurship lesson, one she would carry with her into her future ventures.

Serena's adventurous nature extended beyond business. She became an experienced backcountry skier, taking physical risks I never would have dreamed of. Once, after her first trip, I picked her up to find her heels bleeding from ill-fitting equipment. When I expressed concern, she dismissed it: 'It's just part of the experience, Mom.'

Anneka's professional journey began right after she graduated from Stanford in 2010. She told us she would work for a startup and live in San Francisco. She started at a company called LiveRamp (earlier 'RapLeaf'), and in 2017, after an acquisition and spin-offs, Anneka became the co-CEO of LiveRamp. She insisted she didn't want to be the sole CEO, preferring a partnership where one executive focused on sales while she ran everything else—engineering, product, and operations. It was a massive job, but the company thrived under her joint leadership.

In 2018, LiveRamp's IPO took place at the New York Stock Exchange. Anneka was right there on the podium for ringing the bell. I never had that during my own IPO. Anneka was only thirty years old, but she never seemed caught up in status or ego. She stayed focused, pragmatic, and incredibly organized, managing complex situations with a calm, analytical approach.

Three years later, she resigned. LiveRamp's market capitalization dropped by $500 million. At home, we joked, 'Now we know what our daughter is worth.' In reality, her personal market cap exceeded the market value of Digital Link at many points in its history. I was proud, awed, and deeply impressed.

If you ever want to understand a person's impact on an organization, look at the farewell messages they receive. When Anneka left LiveRamp, her colleagues described her as 'a trusted mentor in and outside of LiveRamp', 'an authentic, fearless, and inspiring leader', and someone with 'intellect and leadership where anyone crossing your path knows what a deep-down person you are.'

After leaving LiveRamp, Anneka joined Rubrik, a cybersecurity company, which went public three years later. In 2024, she was at the podium again for ringing the bell as their chief product officer. Two IPOs by the age of thirty-six.

The Daughter's Strength

WHEN ANNEKA FIRST JOINED RUBRIK IN JULY 2021, TIMES got turbulent. She became pregnant with her first child after they'd just bought a new home, and she was stepping into a fast-growing organization with ambitious plans.

Then, in December 2021, Naren passed away. Suddenly Anneka became the de facto decision-maker in our family at a time when I was struggling with grief and totally shattered.

Back home, she took charge of funeral arrangements, quietly handling tasks I couldn't. Digging through Naren's computer, she pulled up contacts, sent invitations to 150 friends and family, coordinated flowers, food, logistics, and found a photographer—all without asking me to lift a finger.

The most meaningful part for me was the slideshow she created of Naren's vacation photos. He had been the family photographer, capturing thousands of moments over the years. Anneka, with the help of Ashok Uncle and Serena, carefully selected just the right images to bring us back to old, happy times, celebrating his life through the moments he cherished most. Thoughtful as always, Anneka ensured Serena was involved, making sure she never felt sidelined.

Anneka was also the one who made the final decision on how to transport Naren's remains—whether by private plane or commercial flight. I hesitated, overwhelmed. Anneka saw my pain and calmly said, 'Mom is coming back with us, and Dad's body will follow. That's not nearly as important.' She added, 'Right now, the most important thing is that we all stay together.'

If I'd been thinking clearly, such decisions would have been obvious. But in those days, even simple choices felt impossible. I was so grateful for her strength.

After the funeral, I found myself drowning in estate paperwork: banking issues, credit cards, missing passwords. Anneka took a day off work and came over. 'Mom, if managing finances is too much, I'll handle them for you,' she said.

To help me navigate the future, she created a spreadsheet titled 'List of Things to Do,' sorting out tasks when I wasn't capable of organizing them myself. What amazes me is that she did all this while suffering with morning sickness, starting a new job at Rubrik, and grieving her father. She was only thirty-three, carrying an immense load without faltering.

Despite her success, Anneka remains unaffected by material wealth. Her husband, Sean, is a stay-at-home dad who manages most of the parenting, allowing her to focus on her career. They met in Stanford's physics class—he aced it while she struggled. Sean joined a geeky family, and we became five geeks. (Well, four, when Naren jumped off.)

When they married, they rejected an extravagant Indian wedding, opting for an intimate ceremony with just 120 guests—modest by Indian wedding standards, where three to five hundred people is the norm. Anneka's engagement ring, designed by Sean himself, was simple, a stark contrast to the luxury she could afford. For her wedding jewelry, she refused new pieces, choosing instead to wear heirlooms passed down from her grandmothers.

Later the next year, we attended Warren Buffett's Berkshire Hathaway annual shareholders meeting in Omaha and visited Borsheim's, Berkshire's jewelry store. Anneka fell in love with a pair of diamond earrings. I offered to buy them as a belated wedding gift. She accepted at first—but three days later, she returned them to me.

'Mom, I can't accept these. I don't want something from you that I can't buy myself.' I was disappointed, but her reasoning touched my heart. I quietly accepted the gift back and returned it.

Serena's Uncharted Course

SERENA, ON THE OTHER HAND, IS A TRUE BERKELEYITE. She dares to be unconventional. Serena moved between a few startups, and she also pursues daring physical challenges—backcountry skiing, hiking, and mountain climbing. She is purposeful in her endeavors. She volunteered to teach Girls Who Code in Oakland, driving from San Francisco to Oakland with pizzas every weekend for several years.

I see a restless spirit in her, a drive that reminds me of myself. When I once asked her what she wanted to be when she grew up, she didn't hesitate: 'I want to be the boss.' Now, she's making that childhood dream a reality. Recently, she quit her job without a plan to start her own company in AI. It's in the Silicon Valley air, as they say.

Our daughters have shown me there are many roads to success. I, growing up as a woman in India, had very few choices. They have grown up in America, and their formative years were shaped by American education, ethics, and a direct approach to life. The comfort and wealth in which they grew up—unlike us—has not touched them. They are caring and courteous young women who are living purposeful lives. They both work hard. Seeing them as grown-ups now, all my doubts while raising them have vanished into thin air. Like my mother, I, too, want my daughters to have full professional and family lives.

They're writing their own stories now.

Conclusion

MY LIFE WASN'T EASY OR HARD. SOMETIMES IT WAS JOYFUL, sometimes it was painful, but it always moved forward. A steady rhythm of showing up, figuring things out, and just doing—often without a roadmap. Whether it was switching schools across India, learning American culture, crossing picket lines for job interviews, starting a tech company when few women did, prevailing over serious family health issues, or embracing life after business, it was all part of the same cycle: adapt, learn, move forward, work hard.

I was lucky. Nothing was handed to me, but I had people and moments that lifted me: a mother who demanded equal chances for her daughters; an unflappable husband who considered nothing to be a 'big deal' and helped me navigate crises with calm and wisdom; teachers and mentors who nudged me in the right direction; and the chance to build something no other Indian woman had: to take a company public and lead it as CEO.

The IPO wasn't simply about financial success; it represented my full arrival into a world that had only recently opened to people like me. I had moved from being an outsider to someone comfortable in both Silicon Valley's innovation-driven ecosystem and Wall Street's rigorous, demanding financial world.

And while I've had a full professional life and a second career as a semiprofessional bridge team owner, I've also had the joy—and the chaos—of having a remarkable family. Balancing both worlds isn't easy. But it is one-hundred per cent worth it. I love my family more than anything. There were days when I thought I would lose my mind—anyone who's tried to juggle kids, caregiving, and high-stakes meetings on the same day knows what I mean. But there was never a moment when I wished for a different life. I didn't do everything perfectly—not even close—but I never stopped trying.

I didn't expect to be the first Indian woman to take a company public in the United States. I didn't expect to fall in love with bridge. I didn't expect half the turns this life has taken. But I'm grateful for every one of them. Not because they made me extraordinary, but because they made me more of who I am.

Acknowledgments

This memoir is a chronicle of my lived experiences, emotions, and reflections, but it would not have come together without the help of

ALEX SALKEVER, who provided an excellent initial manuscript for this memoir. I learned from him how to weave a story, to make it interesting. His dedication in shaping the narrative truly set the stage for the book.

VERONICA ESCAMEZ, my assistant, whose prodding and encouragement kept me going through the long journey of writing this memoir. Her immense dedication to her own nonprofit, which she has run for the past twenty years, is truly inspiring.

VIVEK WADHWA, a dear friend, author, and renowned technical journalist. Fifteen years ago, Vivek opened the doors to the world of writing for me through Arianna Huffington's *HuffPost*. He selflessly made himself available and introduced me to numerous resources that helped shape my path to becoming an author.